Hidden Treasures

Wrestling with Significance, Faith, and Suffering While Serving in the Developing World

Jennifer Zilly Canales

VIDE

VIDE

Vide Press
6200 Second Street
Washington D.C. 20011
www.VidePress.com

ISBN: 978-1-954618-02-2 (Print)
ISBN: 978-1-954618-03-9 (ebook)

Cover by Miblart.com

Printed in the United States of America

This, my first published work, is dedicated to my parents (all four of them), my loving husband, and the twelve treasures I have been given the privilege to help raise.

Introduction

Have you ever felt deeply unsatisfied with life, like some unnamable thing was missing? How has your own path been marked with suffering and a search for answers? Have you lost a loved one, endured years of chronic illness, or stared death in the face? Have you ever been moved to compassion or longed to make a difference in the world? Have you wondered if God exists and, if so, what He might be like or expect of you?

If you are not a person of prayer and do not believe in God, let me say that I am so glad that you have this book in your hands. *Please keep reading.* My goal is not to preach to the choir but rather to share the rawness of my own questions and struggles while illustrating a few of the answers I've found along the journey.

I was an interdisciplinary studies major in college, and this book likewise is interdisciplinary: it crosses into various realms, from integral orphan care to the devastating effects of police unresponsiveness to cross-cultural marriage. We will jump from intentional minimalist living to biblical hope to child-rearing and back again. Other themes to be explored in this book through the lens of deep personal experience are: the path toward bilingualism, living for something greater than oneself, and the reality of poverty and suffering in today's world. Hopefully at least one of these themes will prove enlightening to you or directly applicable to the life you already lead. My goal is to serve as a small, flickering light along your path.

I must say before we begin that I am keenly aware of my many rough edges; without a doubt there is still much work to be done in me. As I lay my heart bare in this book, I do so not as someone who has "arrived" and has all the answers, but as a simple (and still young) pilgrim who has dared to ask God to lead the way. As my various insecurities and faults appear plain before you, I would ask — if you are a person of prayer — to remember me before the Lord and ask that He might grant me each day a greater measure of wisdom.

This journey of faith and obedience that will unfold on the ensuing pages has not been without its cost. Almost all of my close relationships have dissolved due to distance and disconnect, and I nearly lost my husband when he was kidnapped and tortured by a local gang. Our cattle were stolen, and a dear neighbor of ours was stoned to death a short distance from our home. We have done without certain material luxuries that many take for granted, and our access to water, electricity, and internet have been inconsistent. We've had to surrender our dream of legally adopting our children after years of trying, waiting, and getting nowhere; and we have extended our hand in compassion to those in need only to see many refuse help and openly choose to keep suffering.

In many ways our story has not been one triumphant leap after another, up some imaginary ladder of success and glory, but rather a truly blessed yet grueling death march as we follow Jesus — struggling to give up our own egos, plans, and pleasures in exchange for His perfect will for our lives. This may sound gruesome and even appalling to some, but we trust in the joys that await on the other side of these current trials.

. . .

Recently my mother and stepfather were stranded in our rural home for much longer than they had planned due to the global Coronavirus pandemic. What they intended to be a punctual three-night visit on foreign soil turned into an uncertain two-week epic.

One sunny afternoon during their stay, my stepfather and I sat under the shade of a large tree near the front gate of our ranch where my husband and I live and serve. We had just finished a short walk together. Our cows' pasture extended before us and the beautiful mountainous landscape towered behind us. Somehow the topic of this book — which at the time was nothing more than a small, persistent idea in the back of my mind — came up, and I will never forget what my stepfather said to me. After having expressed my inhibitions in regard to laying my heart bare for the whole world to read, he calmly commented, as if to put me at ease more than to convince me of anything, "Really the book would be about God's heart through your heart, the story of what you all have lived on this ranch."

Upon hearing the simplicity and humility of his remark, something within me clicked and I suddenly felt an unspoken permission, a divine nudge to finally begin compiling this book after so many years of hesitancy. From within my bones I sensed a permeating conviction that seemed to say, *Now's the time.*

After many bouts with tropical illnesses, chronic insomnia, and daily hardships on foreign soil, with fear and trembling I have finally put pen to paper (or rather fingers to my laptop's keyboard) to share our perspective from the trenches. After countless occasions of lying connected to IVs on that old floral-print bed in our rundown local clinic, I trust the Lord has been preparing and humbling me for this moment of sharing with the world our small, yet not insignificant story.

So, I am stepping out in faith to share the tale of God's heart through ours on these seventeen acres, although the journey will inevitably take us into surrounding neighborhoods and cities on occasion. Some of the accounts you will read may cause you to laugh out loud; others might upset you and lead you to disagree with me fundamentally; while I hope others will incite you to deep reflection about the purpose of life and the existence of God.

A Él sea toda la gloria.

A Patchwork Family is Born

November 15, 2013

My husband Darwin and I, accompanied by a dear friend of ours, were waiting anxiously for the first children to arrive at our ranch home. The three of us would embark together on the daily journey of loving and serving in Jesus' name. All three of us had recently moved to our ranch home in rural Honduras with a burning belief that God had called us to the task of raising the parentless and living in Christian community with one another.

During our weeks of preparation, our dear friend created her own beloved, one-of-a-kind title by which she would grow to be known and loved by the children: 'Tía Tiki', *Tía* meaning *Aunt* in Spanish while *Tiki* is her middle name that reflects her West African heritage. In essence, *Aunt Tiki*. Darwin and I would step into the roles of substitute Dad and Mom upon the children's arrival (here known simply as 'Pa' and 'Ma').

Several weeks of active waiting passed when we finally received a call from the local branch of Honduras' child protective agency: there were two sibling groups available. The agency told us the first sibling group was composed of very small children and toddlers, while the second group included slightly bigger children, the eldest being a nine-year-old boy. No family or medical history was given for either sibling group.

All along we were intent on receiving small children between the ages of two and seven years old, because we had been advised repeatedly by the experts that the older a child is, the more baggage he or she has from past traumas and the more difficult it is to cultivate them into healthy, productive individuals.

Upon hearing of the older sibling group, with the nine-year-old boy who clearly fell outside of our safe two-to-seven range, I felt God spoke to my heart and said that we should accept them. This thought raged against reason.

I prayed during the night for confirmation regarding this decision, and the following day received unquestioned support from both Darwin and Tía Tiki.

The next day Darwin and I were away from our ranch home in the city. We don't yet own a car, so our errands were completed via a combination of walking, taking taxis, and riding less than hygienic public buses. Darwin and I began crossing the city to reach the run-down, bubblegum-pink government office that had been such a source of frustration and confusion for us during the previous months.

This time, however, we arrived with hope and anticipation bursting forth in our hearts. Today we might meet our future children; today might be the first day on that long, sacred path the Lord has called us to.

Although my husband and I may never choose to have our own biological children, I dare to compare our experience that sunny afternoon with the emotional sensation I imagine a biological mother feels at childbirth. I felt on the verge of tears. The period of waiting was about to be over in one fell blow; I sensed that the events of the day promised to change our lives forever.

We entered the rusty gate and exchanged friendly greetings with the compound's watchman. Most businesses and government buildings here have armed guards due to such pandemic violence exacerbated by police unresponsiveness. This dilapidated complex of unimpressive one-story buildings was no exception.

Now within the perimeter, I saw them sitting, all three in a row — biggest, middle, then smallest. The three siblings seemed strangely different than the rest of the dozens of energetic children darting about the complex's outdated play area. I made eye contact with the oldest, a girl, and I think she smiled — or maybe only I did! — and I immediately sensed God spoke to my heart: *She will be your daughter.*

This realization hit me like a train, and I thought, *But how?* The government agency said that the oldest child in our potential sibling group, the nine-year-old, was a boy...

I stopped the tidal wave of mental protestations and chose to wait and trust what I believed was God's whisper. We were immediately whisked into the director's office. A cacophony of children's voices ringing throughout the complex, the director looked frazzled and barely greeted us before disappearing.

He had muttered something about bringing the three children he had told us about by phone as he slipped out the door. However, in the depth of my heart I knew (or perhaps only hoped) that the smiling girl and her two younger siblings would return with him.

Soon enough the door to the office swung open, and there they stood awkwardly: *she* and her two younger siblings. My heart leapt as the middle sister stole several shy, toothy grins at my husband and me.

After a bit of searching, we were pleased to find a somewhat private spot where we could get to know the kids. It was quickly established that the oldest was the official spokesperson for the younger two. Although small physically possibly due to malnutrition, the eldest informed us that she was thirteen years old. I became light-headed and nearly gasped. ¡Trece años! How could we possibly take in a teenager? She's only ten years younger than myself! We're looking for kids who are between the ages of two and seven...

But those thoughts rapidly disappeared as my husband and I sensed God was calling us to obey and to have open hearts. We had been informed that the majority of the nation's small children, after all, were already being actively cared for by other foster families and children's homes. The older children and teenagers were the group that was in most desperate need of a chance at family and stability.

After an hour of talking with the three kids and the older local woman who had been caring for them temporarily, Darwin and I said our warm goodbyes. The children stood behind their beloved elderly caregiver and watched us with intense interest as we smiled at them.

We slid back into the director's office and asked what we needed to do to bring the three treasures home. The sibling group had suffered a tragic past and was currently without contact with their biological relatives. They were in need of a permanent, loving home, and that was just what we longed to give them.

Later that day, my husband and I walked back across town through hot, busy city streets to reach the overcrowded public bus terminal where dozens of buses came and went in all directions. We quickly identified the sixteen-passenger van that would take us back to our town just beyond city limits. We jumped aboard, squeezed in tight among sweaty bodies as many more than sixteen passengers crammed into the small space. We traveled, subjected to blaring bus music. The wind whipped my hair through an open bus window and rivers of thanksgiving flowed through my heart. To say that moment was laced with ecstatic joy would have been a vast understatement.

Once back home on our ranch homestead, Tía Tiki and
I triumphantly ripped the plastic coverings off the new mattresses
in the kids' rooms, dressed the beds in age- and gender-appropriate
bedding, fluffed the second-hand pillows, and braced ourselves for our
worlds to be turned upside-down.

Queen Bee, Fireball, and *Shadow Puppet* became part of our
patchwork family the very next day, a mere four months and one
week after my husband and I said our wedding vows.

Rewind:
The Backstory

Summer 1990 — Fall 2007

I might have gotten ahead of myself. Let's rewind a decade or two.

As a little girl growing up in the Texas suburbs, I knew my parents could not have any more children. They had carefully explained that my mother had given birth to me, her firstborn, at age thirty and in budding health, but with the birthing experience came serious implications for her. Upon delivery, she was shuttled into an emergency procedure to remove her uterus due to excessive bleeding. She recovered just fine, but my parents' hope of having two or three children went out the window in one fell swoop. I was destined to be an only child.

Faith was not discussed in our home nor did we pray together as a family, although my mom did attend a local church nearly every Sunday and faithfully took me along with her. Church was the only place where I learned about Jesus, although most Sundays I admittedly forgot my Bible at home. As many around the globe, throughout my childhood I held very little concept of what it truly meant to live for God day to day or what role He could possibly play in a person's life beyond the church walls.

However, from a very young age I believe He planted within me the burning desire to be family to orphaned and abandoned children, which is a topic very close to the biblical God's heart. The Bible tells us time and again that God is Father to the fatherless and has deep compassion for the widows and those who suffer. In my childhood, however, this reality was lost on me. All I knew was that I longed for my parents to adopt.

In elementary school, this desire manifested itself through my repeated attempts to convince my parents (unsuccessfully) to adopt children from the local foster system. With my wild, brown curls and tomboy-like spunk, I was convinced that our home had sufficient space to include more children and that the children's arrival would likewise fulfill my parents' dream of having a larger family. *Talk about killing two birds with one stone.*

One year gave way to the next, however, and my reality of being an only child in a very large two-story home complete with a backyard swing-set and golden retriever never changed.

In high school during the first decade of the new millennium, I remember stumbling upon a Guideposts magazine (a Christian publication) and leafing through its contents disinterestedly. Much to my surprise, a short story about a married couple who decided to adopt two older children caught my eye and ensnared my heart, effectively rekindling the then-dormant desire to form part of an adoptive family. I read and re-read the article as it deeply moved me, my eyes glued to the family photo of the children happy to be loved in their new family.

The dream of my parents adopting had been fading progressively, as they were nearing their divorce. The ardent desire to adopt, however, stirred within me in increasing measure. I decided in that moment that I would adopt as an adult. It looked like I would never have adopted siblings, but I believed it within my reach to become an adoptive mother someday.

It All Started With a Cup of Water

February 25, 2014

Almost four months have passed since that blessed day in November that we welcomed Queen Bee, Fireball, and Shadow Puppet into our previously well-ordered lives.

And, surprisingly enough, the Lord has changed our plans yet again. It all started with a cup of water about a month ago.

Martian Child, our newest treasure, arrived on our ranch several weeks ago as one of the young cowboys who brings a local man's herd to our fields to graze.

As I saw the young boys from a distance, I recalled Jesus' words that we are to give to those in need, and that if we give even a cup of water to a thirsty person in His name, we will participate in God's blessing.

I went to our kitchen and filled up two plastic cups of water for the boys, walked across our ranch property to where they were sitting idly, greeted them kindly, asked their names, dropped off the water, and left. After that I didn't think much more about the incident.

A couple nights later at dinner, Tía Tiki asked nonchalantly, "You remember Martian Child, one of the young cowherders?"

She continued, surprising us by the connection she had evidently established with our young neighbor, "Well, I was talking with him and it looks like he wants to enter our homeschool program. *Está muy interesado en aprender.*"

I felt like a train hit me, and my immediate thought was, *No.* In my narrow-mindedness, I wondered why my dear friend had invited a virtual stranger into our homeschool program that we had been planning explicitly for our three foster children. Why did she have to be so friendly and constantly reach out to strangers, mixing herself around in their personal lives? Her loving extroversion was a quality I had long admired in her (because I myself do not possess this gift), but it likewise inconvenienced and intimidated me.

After a couple of days, the Lord changed my heart and we decided to try to find the eager young Martian Child to talk with him. We discovered he hadn't been in school for some time, which is tragically common in our rural town, especially among older children and teenagers.

I felt way out of my comfort zone even considering the idea of accepting him as a student. I was still adapting to being a new wife and mother to three children! Were we ready to begin expanding our little homeschool into a ministry to local youth?

In my first phone conversation with Martian Child's stepmother, she informed me rather abrasively that she would prefer that her stepson move in with us. She told me that his biological mother abandoned him at the age of two months and that his father died last year during a dangerous circus act (literally), leaving her, his stepmother, in charge of raising him and her three other young children. She worked long hours baking and then selling *tamales* on public buses and struggled to feed her family. Wayward Martian Child was a burden she could no longer shoulder.

Heart pounding, I told her that we would be in touch regarding her stepson's *schooling*, trying to politely ignore her comment about him living with us. I promptly ended the conversation, sweating profusely.

That night I did not sleep as I sensed Jesus' words resonating in my mind, knocking on the door of my heart: *I oftentimes come in disguise — as a street person, as an orphan, as the lowliest of the low — and if you open the door, if you love these outcasts in accordance with My Word, you are actually loving Me. And if you reject them, you are rejecting Me.*

I tossed and turned, trying desperately to find a reason to close our door — *close our hearts* — to Martian Child, this young man whom we barely knew. After all, we weren't planning on receiving more children into our family for about a year, and especially not a twelve-year-old boy. Oh, I wasn't ready for the world of parenting a young man on the cusp of adolescence in the same household as two blossoming females!

The next day we carefully considered our pending decision. Although it was not a plan that birthed from any of our personal plans, we believed that God had placed Martian Child in our path, and that accepting him into our patchwork family would be more than an act of charity or even a risky move; it would be a step of faith borne out of obedience.

So, we jumped through all the necessary hoops at the child protective agency to have Martian Child officially form part of our family. One more treasure was added to the chest. And, as an unexpected bonus, six-year-old Shadow Puppet's typical nighttime fears were abated, and he slept soundly knowing he finally had a roommate.

Memorable Anecdote

Pint-sized Shadow Puppet's written prayer for his future wife:

God, protect my future wife from evil, from the Devil's lies and from robberies. God, protect my future wife so that she doesn't focus only on outside beauty.

180 Degree Turn

Spring 2008

At age seventeen and on the cusp of graduating with honors from a large public high school in San Antonio, I could no longer ignore the numbing void that engulfed my carefree teenage life. I took careful inventory, and I couldn't shake the disturbing sensation that my life had been constructed on a lie, an illusion.

Almost everything I did began to seem utterly pointless. As I looked within myself, I could see there was little of real substance there. Much of my laughter was empty; much of my talk was vain. I had no set compass guiding my life and decisions.

I had all the general material comforts and luxuries any teenager could hope for; both my parents (albeit divorced) loved me dearly; I was highly involved in my school's varsity basketball team, had a wonderful group of friends, and even served as a dedicated volunteer at a local animal shelter. I was accepted to all six colleges I applied to, and it seemed I had every possibility imaginable within my reach.

And, in spite of it all, I felt miserable and in desperate need of real answers, a solid foundation on which to build my future. *Did life have any purpose at all beyond fitting in and following the current around me? What could possibly be missing? Didn't I already have everything that most aspire to? There must be more.* While I believe it common (and necessary) for the human race to confront these existential questions, I am sadly aware that many try to drown out or cover up the void within them with things like drugs and alcohol, violence and hatred, addictions to technology, or even a change of sexual orientation (among other things).

I've heard it said that we all have a "God-shaped hole" within us, and through my searching I've come to firmly believe this. When we do life by our own rules, deep down we can't escape feeling like some unnamable thing is missing, is just beyond our reach. We have all the things that the world says will make us happy, but we feel like we have nothing at all. (Is this why some of the wealthier nations around the globe have such high suicide rates? I suspect the world has lied to us: money can't satisfy us after all.) Many don't see it for what it is; I'm convinced it's the "God-shaped hole", and only He can fill it. *Why?* Because He designed us with the need for communion with Him, and without it we'll never truly be complete.

So, after several months of silent frustration during my Senior year of high school, I finally began reading the Bible page after page for the first time in my life (although not without great difficulty and resistance at first). By God's grace, I sensed deep down that if there were answers to be had, the ancient book must contain them. I began in the Gospel of Matthew, as I longed to learn more about Jesus. If He was who He claimed to be, then I knew the priorities that governed my life had to change drastically. Although I continued going to church with my mom from time to time, God was not in charge of my life and decisions. *I was.*

I spent months reading the Scriptures and other Christian literature on my own and seeking meaning and answers with considerable levels of anguish. Sensing God had been pursuing me, I finally humbled myself, accepting God's sovereignty and forgiveness through the blood of Christ, and gave my life to the Lord. I was a new creation, and I was determined to learn to live as one.

And, just like the man in the biblical narrative who found a hidden
treasure in a field and joyfully sold everything he had to gain the
treasure, I longed to do the same. I longed to forsake the world
in its wild scramble for money and power in order to gain Christ.
I planned to trade in my old life for something much greater from
the hand of the King, a hidden treasure of sorts. I wanted to know
God and live for Him, something that was as foreign to me at the
time as Honduran *montucas* are to the typical American.

Missing the Point

April 23, 2014

We have now been on this wild ride of parenthood a little over six months, and it indeed has more sharp, majestic peaks and rapid descents into scary valleys than the best roller coasters the world has to offer. We would not change our children for the world, but neither can we deny the unforeseen challenges we've come up against. Many days my goal has been nothing more noble than mere survival. Many of our children's past traumas are still being played out daily in behaviors that make me want to run away, dig a hole in the dirt, and bury my head as any alarmed ostrich would do.

And, in the midst of this intense learning curve, many of my own unhealthy behaviors have also been brought unexpectedly to light.

Recently I listened attentively as our child psychologist explained Fireball's pencil-sketch she made of me hand-washing laundry. "That can be a sign that she sees you as compulsive, as being more interested in tasks than in being attentive to the people in your life. *Su hija revela sus sentimientos a través de sus dibujos.*"

Although we hadn't been in agreement with everything our psychologist had said up until that point (nor do we believe that a psychologist should be the main agent in healing a person's broken past; that is God's job), this time I knew in my heart that he was right.

This overachieving urge to *go* and *do*, although many times it is in Jesus' name and for the intended benefit of blessing others, has led me to a season of almost constant stress. Many ideals and false conceptions about service to the poor have been stripped from me in these past several months. All around me I see so much need. We venture down that rocky road littered with trash into our rural town and see so many broken lives; I do not know where to start, how to help them properly. Tía Tiki actively exercises her gift of evangelism and proves a wise friend and source of encouragement to many locals. My husband Darwin and I try to be intentional about serving and praying where we can, but it never seems like enough. The scope of whatever influence we have is greatly limited. Life here is complicated and messy, and easy answers just don't suffice.

And, as hard as it is to admit, many times I've found a momentary refuge or distraction in *doing* — cleaning, organizing, and so on as little Fireball's drawing so accurately depicted — *anything* so as not to face head-on the reality of suffering around me.

Yes, we have countless honest neighbors, and hard-working families abound in our humble rural town. Many women plant flowers in their front yards, and little churches can be found sprinkled about the rocky landscape. People generally respond positively to a friendly greeting as they cross paths on the street, and many families will make great sacrifices to ensure their children get a decent education. Many extended family members have honorably given themselves to the task of raising their grandchildren, nieces, and nephews when these would have otherwise ended up homeless. There are many driven Hondurans here trying to make a difference among their people, but it would be naïve to ignore the fact that there are also deep, dangerous currents of apathy and anarchy to be fought against.

One biblical passage that we read frequently with our children is Jesus' radical call not to worry — about clothes, food, drink, or what tomorrow may bring. I often become frustrated when the children don't "get it." When they still worry about food or have seventy-three questions about what we are going to do tomorrow. When they place too much importance on clothes and appearance. *But they know Jesus' command and say they want to be His followers,* I think with disappointment.

In all of this time, however, I, more than anyone else, have missed the point. I have had my gaze too intently fixed on the preoccupations of tomorrow, have fretted endlessly about next month's finances, or tried to peek fearfully into what next year might bring. I have secretly allowed worry to eat away at my gut, trying to take matters into my own hands rather than accepting the call to trust God fully.

Several mornings in the last few weeks, I have felt God calling me to rise early, to find Him in the still, quiet hours in order to reverse the trend of anxiety. I have oftentimes stood on our porch in amazement during the chilled, tranquil mornings, a very tangible sense of awe sweeping over me as I look out at the mist covering the mountain range behind our home. The birds of paradise begin their early calls; another perfect day spills forth from the heart of the Creator. I ask God for the strength to love well and to be fully present both to Him and to those precious treasures He's placed in my life.

Memorable Anecdote

Preteen Martian Child in a hand-written letter to 'Ma':

I consider you to be my real mom. Thank you for letting me live with you and Pa. God has given me a room to sleep in. Thank you for planning to celebrate my birthday. Thank you, Ma, for giving me a hug every day. I love you so much.

 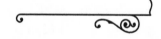

Establishing
a New Identity

Fall 2008 — Spring 2012

A few short months after my high school graduation I moved over 600 miles away to begin my university studies at a small liberal arts school in Arkansas. My plan: learn to establish a new identity in Christ in an environment totally removed from all that I previously knew. I was conscious of the fact that my walk with the Lord would have to be fought for and would not occur magically or instantaneously. (Oh, how many people "give their lives to the Lord" in a brief moment of prayer only to then fall away from the faith so soon after the initial emotion fades!) I was constantly on alert not to fall back into easy, known patterns that I had enjoyed in my earlier life. I trusted God had something better in store beyond seeking acceptance and happiness through buying, saying, and doing the "right" things and generally living for "me."

Multitudes of things were still unknown to me, but one thing I clung to: I believed God was calling me to something beyond what the general population experiences or chooses, and I would live that new lifestyle with and for God.

Throughout my college years I actively participated in the few campus faith activities that were available in the midst of what was generally a non-Christian student (and professor) body. A small group of close friends and I established a weekly Bible study at a local homeless shelter. That old two-story white house not a mile from campus that served as shelter and soup kitchen for many would grow to become my church, the official site where I weekly sought to love as Christ and to grow in His Word alongside others whom I deeply cared for.

Inevitably, at the end of each Bible study I participated in, the leader would ask if anyone had a prayer request they would like to share (as is common in many Christian faith circles around the globe). The longing for wisdom was so overwhelming within me that that — *wisdom* — was quite literally my only prayer request for a period of roughly three years. Those in attendance would just laugh knowingly and eventually stopped asking altogether my weekly prayer request because they already knew what I would say. I had read in the Bible that God promises wisdom to those who ask for it, without doubting, and I was clinging to that promise for dear life. *I longed to be wise according to God's standards, not the world's.*

Our Favorite Neighbor

October 7, 2014

Entering our ranch's kitchen pantry, I bent over to scoop out concentrated feed mix for our chickens from a large burlap sack when I suddenly felt like an invisible fist had been driven hard into my solar plexus, and tears began to flood my eyes.

No, I thought. *Not now, not yet.* I forced the flood gates to close and regained momentary composure, knowing that we would be going to the chicken run together. This would be our last early morning trip together to feed and water our hungry laying hens. Then we would help him pack his bags. And he would move out.

After over eight months of almost constant struggle — sometimes meaningful and profound, fringed with beauty as we saw hints of progress, while at other times so mind-bogglingly frustrating that we wanted to pull our hair out and stomp about like mad men — Martian Child, whom we had taken in and loved as a son, had decided to leave and return to his stepmother's home a short walk away.

I knew we had not withheld any good thing from him, any measure of affection. Foot massages, singing him to sleep at night. We did not forget to say, "I love you" or *"Estamos orgullosos de ti."* Oh, how many hundreds of times did we say those things!

During that last morning together, I didn't scold him for having done things poorly or for what we perceived as laziness and ungratefulness. I didn't nag, nor did I try to convince him to stay.

Rather, I gently held his face in my hands, his eyes drilling mine with an intensity I had yet seen from him. We stood there, in the kitchen he and I, for over an hour. He listened intently as I believe the Lord spoke through me; I myself had no more to give.

This tough guy who never cries, who guffaws when he's nervous and pokes fun at others to hide his own insecurities, who only this year learned how to properly read and write, had tears welling up in his eyes, as I did cascading over my heart.

As my fingers tousled his short, silky hair, I asked, "Do you want to go with me to the chicken run before we help you pack your stuff? *Las gallinas tienen hambre."* For us it seemed like the perfect ending to this little, seemingly insignificant chapter in God's overarching redemption of mankind.

Martian Child accepted with a smile, and off we went as if it were any other day.

God, this hurts so bad. I'm scared of what he'll find beyond our gate. Please protect him; transform him in ways we were unable to. My heart prayed silently as we walked together.

Even in the midst of my own heartbreak, I knew that it all boils down to freedom. God grants that freedom — *free will* — to each one of us. He does not force our hand or try to manipulate our decisions. He is saddened when His children choose the world over Christ, and He longs for their repentance, their return. There are consequences for how we use our freedom, of course, and when we stand in front of His throne at the end of our lives those consequences will prove eternal and irreversible, but we will have no one to look to beyond ourselves, for it is we who decided how to use the delicate freedom entrusted to us.

Likewise with Martian Child. As he and I tended to our hungry laying hens that morning, I ruminated on the fact that we had earnestly tried for months to convince him to be a productive, joyful member of both our temporal family and God's eternal one, but ultimately it is and always was *his choice*. In respecting his right to choose, we affirm God's role in allowing all humanity the same.

So now Martian Child is our favorite neighbor, and we still see him nearly every day, either on our ranch or in our town. We go to his stepmother's home periodically to check up on him, and through this increased contact we're forming a positive relationship with his stepmother.

It is a new season, and we are grateful that we are still granted the privilege of forming part of his life, albeit now less intensely.

One More
Spanish Class

Fall 2009 - Spring 2012

My college experience also opened the doors to bilingualism, something I had never dreamt of or thought possible for my life. In my second semester of university-level Spanish, I had the privilege of being in the class of a phenomenal professor who opened my heart and mind to new horizons. His sharp wit and signature waxed mustache (yes, it curled up on the ends) intimidated some while captivating others. Surprisingly (and initially against my own will), I had found excitement in learning all the verb tenses, vocabulary words and grammatical structures presented in that little lecture hall. At the end of the semester the professor pulled me aside and encouraged me to keep going, to take *one more* Spanish class and to consider legitimately pursuing the mastery of a second language.

My knee-jerk reaction was to laugh good-naturedly, as that second-semester class was enough to fill my foreign language requirement. I was done; I had fulfilled my academic duty.

However, after carefully considering my favorite professor's challenge, I decided to sign up for *one more* class the following semester, this time not to check off a course requirement but because I had decided to go after bilingualism seriously.

Over the ensuing years of college, the doors were opened to study abroad. My dream had always been to go to Africa, Eastern Europe, or Asia, but a series of events and a few sharp words of wisdom from my mentor led me to explore Latin America. The logic was simple, and my beloved mentor's words served as a large flashing arrow placed strategically along my path: "Jennifer, you're already learning Spanish. Pursue it further. You don't speak a lick of French or Romanian or Thai. Dig deeper the well that is already under construction; perfect one second language rather than dabbling in several."

I was hesitant at first, but eventually accepted the inevitable: I would be going to Latin America and not to some other destination that for unknown reasons seemed more appealing. I went to Nicaragua for a semester and then studied abroad in Argentina. I didn't fall in love with Latin American culture, but I sure was learning a lot of Spanish. And it was in Argentina, after all, that I met Tía Tiki, who would later move to Honduras to serve as our children's hilarious aunt and faithful friend.

My Spanish-English dictionary, a Spanish grammar guide, and a verb conjugation book were my constant companions throughout my Latin American travels, and I made a daily effort to look up new words, underline relevant material in my books, and practice verbally my communication skills (however poorly it all came out at first).

Lo and behold, after years of dogged effort (and much initial resistance on my part), the reality of bilingualism was dawning on the horizon. *One more class* had turned into a demanding yet highly rewarding journey of three years.

The Man With The Whipping Rope

October 27, 2014

Recently, I was in the city to do some errands and then use the internet at a local café as we do not have internet access on our ranch. I first stopped by my favorite breakfast spot — an old wooden cart parked alongside the curb in one of the city's busy downtown streets. Taxis, buses, cars, cyclists, pedestrians, and emaciated street dogs passed by as a few women prepared *baleadas* over several gas-powered burners. They flipped tortillas on the skillet with their bare hands. People of all walks of life stood in line to place their orders.

That morning as I sat on one of about a half dozen plastic chairs lining the busy, narrow sidewalk, eating my breakfast in a small basket on my lap, I became uncharacteristically uncomfortable with my surroundings. This is not, however, hard to do in the city. Some men whistle and shout inappropriate remarks at women, and in the more crowded areas almost everything tends to have a claustrophobic feel. Vendors' voices call out in all directions, and danger could be lying around any corner.

My eyes landed upon a homeless man with a knotted rope in his hands, talking nonsense and swinging the rope up against the back of someone's parked truck, a sort of semi-soft whipping motion.

A thoroughly unpleasant man from all points of view, I took a quick appraisal of the situation and tried to calculate the risk of being his next whipping victim. My breakfast still in my lap, I mentally readied myself to run at a moment's notice should his whipping rope come flying my way.

I hesitated to leave my plastic chair (knowing that any other sidewalk or park bench nearby would probably have similar surroundings) when suddenly a thought presented itself to me: *I myself am that man.*

Apart from the forgiveness and cleansing blood of Christ, we are all just like that man. Before God we stand in our filthiness, our nonsense, our unpleasant nature.

That dirty, crazy, his-presence-ruins-my-breakfast man; yes, you and I are just like him. In light of God's perfect holiness each one of us falls short of His glory no matter how intelligent, accomplished, or polished we believe ourselves to be. Just because we wear business attire or work in a cubicle or even actively serve in a church does not mean we are innately more pleasing to God than this man. If I think I am better than him because I graduated from college and don't pee in the street and know that whipping a rope against a car is not socially acceptable, I just might be more lost than he is.

God sees us much more clearly than we see ourselves; God knows that man and I are on the same level, both desperately in need of His grace, my sin no better or worse than his. God chose to send His son to die for us — for that man and you and me — not because we deserve it, but because He is merciful.

All of these thoughts appeared in my mind as a landslide, and after finishing my breakfast on that busy downtown sidewalk, I quietly gathered my belongings and went on my way with a new sense of humility and gratefulness weighing on my chest.

Entrusted
with a Vision

Summer — Fall 2011

In 2011, which was indeed my year of almost constant globe-trotting, my dear college roommate and I were selected for a financial grant from our university to walk the *Camino de Santiago* (Way of Saint James), a world-renowned hiking trail that thousands visit from around the globe each year. Historically, it is said to be the path which James from biblical times took in order to spread the Gospel across northern Spain.

My roommate and I lived as "pilgrims" for roughly three weeks, surviving on a diet mainly consisting of French bread (think a long, plain loaf) and olive oil due to our limited personal funds. We walked up to eleven hours per day across Spanish countryside, through countless small towns, and even through a big city or two. Our purpose in doing the famous hike was not merely cultural; we intended to find God along the Way. Our college graduation, after all, would occur within a year's time, and neither of us knew what direction to take afterward. We ardently longed to fulfill God's will for our lives, but we just weren't sure yet what He had in store for us. We were looking for a sign, a clue, and we thought that distancing ourselves from technological connection and the entanglements of daily life for a few weeks just might grant us enough space and inner silence to discern God's voice.

Walking in intermittent silence and then resting in hostels each evening, several books and journals were our constant companions. Mid-June I was sitting cross-legged on the top bunk where I would lie down to sleep later that night. The open hiking backpack my stepmother had bought me sat at the foot of the mattress, and I rummaged through it until I found my journal.

I glanced across the room to see my dear friend and hiking companion reading her Bible, while a few other "pilgrims" came filtering in and out of our shared sleeping quarters. I grabbed my pen with the intent of jotting down a fresh written prayer, asking God for wisdom and direction over my future, when a vision suddenly and unexpectedly entered my mind's eye.

I do not say this lightly, nor do I say so in an attempt to super-spiritualize my experience or exaggerate reality, but the image that so clearly came to mind in that specific moment — and the accompanying instruction — have so deeply marked my life that I have henceforth allowed that vision (that I earnestly believe was from God) to guide much of my decision-making over the ensuing decade.

What did I see? I was in an old bedroom with brightly colored walls — two blue, two orange — although the paint was noticeably worn and chipping. There were a few rusty metal bunk beds in that room, each with a child — clearly not biologically mine — lying down, ready for bedtime. I was experiencing everything around me as if I were standing there within that little room, seeing everything in real time. Suddenly, I began walking towards the bunk beds and gently tucking in the children, bending over to tend to those on the bottom bunks first. In that moment an undeniable epiphany flashed across my mind, leaving in its wake a burning desire to obey: *Your purpose in My Kingdom will be to be a mother to those who have none.*

That was it, and as quickly as the scene occurred it came to a close. I was left alone, heavenly joy threatening to burst from within and shatter me into a million little pieces right there in that anonymous Spanish hostel. No lightning struck from heaven and no special instruction was written in the stars, but after that decisive moment my life would forever be set apart for the purpose I believe the Lord revealed to me. Adoption had, after all, been a longing of my heart since my early childhood; He had simply confirmed the seed He planted within me so many years ago.

The ensuing months would be filled with prayer and anticipation, this time not for wisdom and a revealing of God's will for my life but rather specific details, guided direction. I believed in my heart of hearts that the Lord spoke to me in that Spanish hostel and permanently fixed the compass of my life, but I longed to know where, with whom, and when.

Would this divine undertaking occur on U.S. soil or in some forgotten corner of the third world? Did the Lord have a husband picked out for me with whom this sacred task would be fulfilled together, or was I to foster or adopt as a single woman (as many valiantly do)?

Armed with the vision the Lord gave me and not much else, one of the new cries of my heart began to be for a *home*, a place to put down roots and to raise the children who would arrive in God's timing. My childhood home and semblance of familial unity, after all, were disintegrated. I loved my parents dearly, but I no longer had a coherent sense of home with them. I had likewise spent a good portion of my college years traveling to different places for summer internships and volunteer projects, not only on foreign soil but also within U.S. borders.

My prayer, then, had transformed from a deep longing for wisdom to an overwhelming desire for a home. *Lord, please show me where my home will be and with whom. I'm willing to go anywhere, but please give me some kind of sign in Jesus' name.*

Didn't See
That One Coming

November 15, 2014

Out here in the Central American boonies, our water system has always been an enigma to me. When we least expect it, there is a problem with our tubing or tank or the town's water supply. Suddenly there is no running water on our property for a couple hours or as long as a couple days.

That means no water for washing dirty dishes and extra costs and hassle in buying large back-up water jugs for drinking. It also means traipsing down to the dwindling stream behind our property to wash clothes, to fill up the farm animals' drinking pails, and maybe even to bathe ourselves.

We are currently in the midst of another rainy season, and a couple weeks ago as my husband, Darwin, was getting ready to travel with our faith community to install a potable water system in a poor rural village several hours away, I found myself complaining about our *own* water system. I was not looking forward to having to jimmy with the valves, check the tubes, and hope the water didn't go out while Darwin was away.

My sweet husband cut me off before I sent out official invitations to my pity party. With a sincere grin on his eternally optimistic face, he outstretched his muscular arms and said, "Hey, we haven't died of thirst yet! *No te preocupes tanto, amor.*"

That is code for: *Jennifer, God has continually provided us with what we need, even if at times it is not convenient or easy. Let's give thanks rather than complain.*

He was right. I chuckled (or rather groaned) wearily and agreed, assuming an inward posture of humble thanksgiving before the Lord.

A few days later, while Darwin was away for his service trip, someone came to our front door. It was our trusted neighbor who weedeats our yard each month, and he came bearing bad news. While weedeating, he accidentally chopped the *entire* PVC pipe that descends from our water tank to provide water to the buildings on our property *in half*.

I serenely followed him to the scene of the accident, certain that what I was about to see wouldn't be pretty. Sure enough, the tube was sliced in half and water was spraying out in all directions, rapidly emptying the tank of our entire source of water. I laughed and thought, *Well, this is new! I certainly didn't see this one coming …* New item to add to my long worry-wort list in regard to our water woes: the possibility of a weedeater gone haywire. *Check.*

I assured our neighbor that mistakes happen, and that God is always good. I thanked him for telling me the truth about the matter and not trying to lie about or cover up what had occurred.

Later that afternoon, as the mountain of dirty laundry called my name, I hauled bucket after bucket on my shoulders down to that knee-deep stream behind our ranch home, marking up my jeans with grass stains in the process. I laughed under the falling rain. As I knelt on the rocky bank, washing our clothes in the cleansing current, I felt that in the most unexpected of ways I was gaining a deeper understanding of how constant God's provision is and how readily available is His peace in the face of potentially trying circumstances.

The Huge Problem With This List

Spring 2012

In that tense last semester of college amidst great levels of uncertainty regarding my future, I had a life-changing meeting with my beloved mentor. As we sat around a small table in a cozy corner of her living room near the back windows, she had instructed me to make a list of all that I hoped and dreamed for the future. I did so fairly speedily and proudly handed her my organized list of ten or so items for her review.

My mentor, a highly educated older woman with a lifetime of valuable personal and professional experiences under her belt, took one glance at my noble aspirations and said in a no-nonsense yet loving tone, "There's a huge problem with this list."

I stared at her blankly, silently fighting off the temptation to be offended and even wounded by her blunt rejection. She had been investing in my life significantly and consistently for the past six years, and she had played a pivotal role in so many of my big decisions. *What problem could she possibly see in my list?*

She continued, "Every aspiration you have begins with 'I.' *I want this; I want that.* Your future should not be about what *you* want, but rather what God wants. What are *His* dreams for you?"

That opened the way for a wonderful discussion around that little table, just her and me in an otherwise silent and immaculately clean house. She proposed to me the idea of moving to Central America to live out the vision I believed God had given me about being an adoptive mother. I could work under the tutelage of a close friend of hers in Honduras with the possibility of staying long-term. My mentor's excitement was genuine, but I was more than reluctant. She informed me that her dear friend had a music school in a Honduran city and was well underway with the construction of an orphanage out in the countryside.

I thought, *I know nothing about music, and my call from God is to be a mother to those who need one, not to work as an orphanage employee.* Even in the limited concepts I held at the time, I knew there was a vast difference between the two. *Parenting* someone suggests the warmth and healing intimacy of a tight-knit, committed family unit; *working at an orphanage* typically includes a rotating staff and oftentimes impersonal relationships with masses of children in an institutional setting. I wanted nothing to do with the latter.

Placing that thought aside, I protested, "But I don't like Latin American culture. I already spent a semester in Nicaragua and another in Argentina because *you* encouraged me to continue learning Spanish. But I didn't enjoy it, nor did I ever feel at home there. Toward the end of my stay in Argentina I couldn't wait to get out of there and vowed I would not be returning to Latin America. *Ever.*"

Upon hearing my honest (yet immature) remarks, my beloved mentor had another choice reprimand for me, albeit in a motherly tone, "Stop that right now. That is extremely selfish and narrow-minded of you to completely mark off an entire section of the globe just because you didn't 'like' your experience there. You need to consider what God's plans are in the midst of all this."

Her frankness (and wisdom) gave me something to think about over the next several days, and I finally decided to reach out to her elderly friend in Honduras to see if there was any dialogue to be had. I sent a brief email to the lady introducing myself and asking a few general questions, hit send on my laptop from the comfort of my college dorm room, and hoped that my message would get lost in cyberspace so that she would never respond.

Little Legs
with Too-Huge Pants

January 30, 2015

Our second Christmas as a family came and went without many bells and whistles, as we've decided not to participate in the general madness of the holiday rush of buying gifts or decorating our home. Our celebration was quiet and simple, as we are fully aware that the celebration of Christ should not occur only on Christmas and Easter but rather as a *daily* celebration (and one which requires obedience) all throughout the calendar year.

Although occurring close to the holiday season but not in response to it, our family did purchase its first vehicle recently from a local dealer, a used 2000 Toyota pickup. It seems that for now our commutes on public busses and our long waits at busy terminals have come to a close. No more hitchhiking adventures for us!

. . .

Yesterday Queen Bee, Fireball, Shadow Puppet, and I held hands in our front yard, eyes closed and hearts racing. We whispered one last prayer as my husband Darwin opened the gate. The government's pickup truck came rumbling onto our property. We would be parents not to three but now to five.

I waved excitedly and smiled although my weary cheek muscles shook slightly. They had been an adrenaline-laced few days of preparation, prayer, and nerves.

The back door of the double-cab opened, and some little legs with pants several sizes too big began reaching precariously for the ground far below.

Broken Boy, six years old. Special needs.

His eleven-year-old sister, *Tender Heart*, was right on his heels, exiting the government vehicle with an impressive display of self-confidence. I had met the two treasures a few days prior as a government social worker was discerning the children's future. Tender Heart's emotional maturity during that initial encounter deeply touched me. She had a unique, delicate quality to her.

I wondered in a blur, *Were we ready for this adventure, this daring new chapter in our patchwork family's story?* We had understood our purpose, after all, as being that of parenting as many as we could, for the need among older children was just so overwhelming. We'd calculated that our 800 square foot cinder block home could comfortably hold up to eight treasures (using bunk beds strategically), so the decision to seek new arrivals had seemed natural and expected. *It was time, wasn't it?*

In spite of my own masked insecurities, it seemed that our three kids believed themselves to be genuinely prepared and even excited to meet the new siblings. I smiled at the three with my eyebrows raised playfully, and we all swooped in for the big welcome.

Broken Boy screamed bloody murder, fearfully eyeing our three friendly dogs who formed part of the welcoming committee. It looked like his eyes would burst out of his sockets. *"Tranquilo, chiquito.* The dogs are our friends," we reassured our frightened new son.

Late in the evening I passed through our living room to see ten-year-old Fireball playing "doctor" with her new little brother. Broken Boy has a severe speech impediment and walks with a limp, but Fireball had enthusiastically set up an entire scene in our living room with feather boas, stuffed animals of all sizes, and a very large doll that was receiving urgent medical attention with "Doctor Broken Boy" for her fever. Fireball was the patient's concerned mother, of course.

It was a sleepless night for Darwin and me, as much due to joyful thanksgiving to our Father as listening for our new treasures to get up or cry. Broken Boy did indeed get up about twenty-five times, repeatedly turning on the light after bedtime and slamming his bedroom door (always with a big, toothy grin). He tried several times to climb the top bunk to be in Shadow Puppet's bed, insisted on wearing his shoes to sleep, and repeatedly jammed his new stuffed animals in his mouth.

It is through this little boy with buckteeth and clothes that aren't the right size that I believe God will teach me what it means to be patient and to love without expecting anything in return.

Memorable Anecdote

A hand-written love note from pint-sized Fireball to her 'Pa' Darwin:

Pa, I consider you to be a good father and a good man, faithful and sincere to my Ma Jennifer. You are an example for everyone to follow, Pa. Thank you for your advice, for guiding me along the right path, and for the way you discipline me. You are a real Christian and a good child of God. I love you a lot. Thank you for having me happily in your home.

A Bizarre Interview

Spring 2012

Well, the email I sent to the elderly missionary in Honduras didn't get a response. Not for five weeks, at least.

After such prolonged silence I had assumed that I would not be receiving a reply from her, and quite honestly, I was relieved to see the days drag on without an email from her. I had, after all, been in increasingly frequent communication with a small faith-based organization in Africa and had great hopes of joining them in their service to the poor after graduation. The lady in Honduras probably didn't even need my help, and as far as I was concerned it was better that way.

Lo and behold, I was waist-deep in fulfilling the last of my graduation requirements when an email appeared in my campus inbox from Teresa Devlin, the veteran missionary who had been serving in Honduras for the past fifteen years.

I opened the message hesitantly, aware that God might destroy my own plans and replace them with His upon doing so. The message was short and left much to be desired. She suggested a phone call to get to know one another further without providing hardly any other information. Remembering the much-deserved scolding I had received from my wise mentor, I promptly answered the elderly missionary. I wasn't expecting much.

Thankfully, she didn't take five weeks to answer my second email.

She called me on the day and time we agreed to, and I braced myself for one of my first real interviews. My palms began sweating as I considered the personal and professional questions she would surely ask. I was twenty-one years old and soon to be released into the world of working adults; I needed to learn to act like one! Although the possibility (or, better yet, *desirability*) of moving to Honduras seemed a far stretch, nonetheless I approached the conversation with butterflies zooming about my gut.

After exchanging a brief greeting, she skipped any polite effort at small talk altogether and entered "interview mode" without taking a second breath. "You know, Honduras is a very dangerous country. It has one of the highest murder rates in the world. Sadly, just recently some local missionaries were killed..."

Confusion and alarm lit up my insides as I dumbly stared at my perfectly grey-colored dorm wall, my old-school flip-phone glued to my ear. *What? Was this her idea of an interview?*

She continued onward, citing an array of internationally-respected data and personal experiences to further illustrate how dangerous Honduras was. My mind spun but I kept listening as I found myself passively participating in this rather bizarre icebreaker. Then, unexpectedly, there was a pause on her end. She ventured in a slow, drawn-out manner, "Well ... what do you think about all of that?"

Groping for the right words for several moments, I finally broke the awkward silence, "Well ... *Yes* ... I'm aware that Honduras is a very dangerous country ... I believe, however, that if God calls me there, He will protect me. But, if He chooses not to and my life is prematurely taken, I trust I will enter His Kingdom–"

Before I could babble anything else, she cut me off with, "*You'll do great here!*" The little woman on the other end of the line exploded with an unprecedented display of enthusiasm. My mouth opened slightly, no sound coming out, as I continued to study the perfectly banal grey wall before me.

She congratulated my point of view ecstatically, and before I knew it, the conversation was over and we had hung up. *She had only asked me that one question in the entire "interview."* I was still not entirely sure what had gone down between us, but I sensed it had been some kind of test (and I had passed with flying colors, much to my own bewilderment). I had even numbly agreed by the end of the conversation to visit her in Honduras during my upcoming Spring Break.

It had, after all, come down to visiting the promising African mission or traveling to see the elderly Teresa Devlin in Honduras during my last Spring Break as a student. Against all logic I had said yes to the old woman with bizarre interview methods in Central America.

Needless to say, my mentor was thrilled; I was not.

Who Pooped in the Burger King Playground?

February 2, 2015

My new special-needs son did. *Poop in the Burger King playground,* that is. We were on Day Three of our parents-to-five adventure, and after going to a couple used-clothing shops to expand our two new arrivals' wardrobe, I took the kids to a special treat that we'd only done one other time — lunch at Burger King in the city and time to explore the big playground inside.

My husband Darwin was on a father-daughter date with Queen Bee that day, so I was with the four younger treasures and everything was going along perfectly. I sat in the playground room, distracted from reading my book as various little people continually stuck their heads out of the big play structure, calling my name to look and wave.

Then something strange happened. Tender Heart, our new eleven-year-old daughter, came over to me and plainly informed, "Jennifer, my brother pooped in his pants. "

I was dumbstruck and could only think to ask, "Does this happen frequently?" Her response: *Sí.*

I put on my metaphorical "momma" pants and said, "Ok, I'll take care of this, Sweetheart. You just keep playing. *¡Diviértete!*" Then I looked down at Broken Boy's big grin and smelly pants and asked myself, *What now?*

The only logical solution seemed to be to walk six-year-old Broken Boy to the women's bathroom and try to clean him up in one of the stalls. As we went hand-in-hand, we left a sporadic trail of smeared poo from the play place to the bathroom as the brown substance dripped down his pant leg and onto the shiny tile floor. Oh, and not to mention the little *mound* of wet poo he left on the scene of the crime within the play place, which I didn't even notice until returning from the bathroom.

He and I squeezed into one of the stalls in the women's bathroom, and after stripping him of his clothes I sat him on the toilet. Seeing as his legs were smeared with poop, the act of sitting him down then transferred — or maybe even multiplied, who knows — a large quantity of the sticky substance onto the priorly squeaky-clean toilet seat. Poop was everywhere!

I remembered in that moment the reality of the "unexplainable peace" that is available to us through Jesus Christ that our missionary mentor had been teaching us about lately. I began to laugh out loud in that little Burger King bathroom stall, uncontrollably joyful as I declared in Spanish to no one in particular, "God is sufficient! *¡Dios es suficiente!*"

So many times we mistakenly think we need God *plus* something else to make us happy. Maybe God *plus* a nice smartphone or God *plus* a comfortable income and benefits or God *plus* kids who behave well and *don't* poop in the Burger King playground.

I realized in that moment that God alone is all that we need. He is enough. Add or subtract anything else — displeasing circumstances, a stellar vacation, a great relationship — and nothing truly changes. If we cannot find contentment in God through Christ, we cannot find it in anything else.

Broken Boy and I eventually walked hand-in-hand *back* to the play area as several customers commented out loud on how bad the restaurant smelled. I think all of the restaurant's janitors were called to the scene, because we passed by more than a couple moppers and disinfectors hard at work to recover the glistening floor that my beautiful new son had so effortlessly spoiled. I had to hold in a giggle and resisted the temptation to laugh out loud and say, "*¡Fuimos nosotros!* My beautiful new son is the one who pooped on your floor! But God is sufficient!"

When we got home that evening, I told my husband Darwin "Today I bought this little backpack for Broken Boy, because from now on whenever we go out with him, we are going to need to take an extra pair of clothes and quite possibly invest in diapers, because *anything* can happen."

The significance of my words seemed utterly lost on my uninitiated husband. I chuckled, adding, "It's a long story; just trust me on this one. *Pero Dios es suficiente.*"

Memorable Anecdote:

A hand-written letter from 'Pa' Darwin to little Fireball:

I want you to know that I love you with a sincere love that expects nothing more than to see you one day soar in Christ like an eagle. Ma Jennifer and I are very thankful to God that He's put you in our lives as our daughter. Your prayers help us a lot, and likewise we pray for you because we know that God has very special plans in store for your future. It is so beautiful to see you now enjoy life without crying for long hours. I cannot imagine our lives with you, Fireball. Thank you for being the way you are.

The Little Melodious Abode

Spring 2012

The pages of my passport increasingly worn, I arrived on Honduran soil during my last Spring Break as a student. Throughout the long day of travel, I was quite conscious of the fact that I was once again in Latin America not because *I* wanted to be, but rather because this might just be *God's* answer for my future.

I sat perched on the twin-sized bed that would be mine for the next few nights, literally inches from elderly Teresa's double-sized bed. We would be the unlikeliest of roommates in the rented one-story yellow house where she lived and directed a small music school in the heart of the city. I had no musical training but enjoyed hearing close to a dozen local students practicing their violins and gaily tapping away on keyboards out in the living room. Their carefree melodies filled that little yellow house and quite possibly the entire block.

Teresa, born in Costa Rica to Central American parents and later raised in the States from age eleven on, was in her early seventies. She had suffered unspeakably over three decades with a debilitating disease called scleroderma and looked small and frail beyond her years. Long, baggy skirt, old lady tennis shoes, and shortly cropped grey hair. I towered when I stood near her, my 5'11" lanky, athletic frame and abounding natural brown curls the stark opposite of her physical condition. Within her, however, was an impressive drive and undeniable faith that could be felt in her presence. I respected her deeply, and I silently hoped she would like and approve of me.

Over the ensuing days, from the intimate position of not only houseguest but *roommate*, I would quietly witness Teresa take dozens of pain-killers and prescription meds in addition to injecting herself each evening before laboriously climbing into her bed so close to mine. She never complained, but her physical pain was palpable. I wondered in awe if I could have served God the way that she had in such debilitating physical condition for so long. I quickly took note of her perseverance and silently asked God to grant me the same for my future.

Knit Together as One Body

February 6, 2015

Sure enough, the day after the infamous Burger King poo parade, my husband got to experience first-hand just what I had gone through. We were at our missionary mentors' home when déjà vu occurred: preteen Tender Heart appeared from around a corner to matter-of-factly inform us that her little brother had pooped in his pants.
I glanced at my husband Darwin who sat beside me on a wooden front-porch bench, and said with a wry smile, "Now it's your turn. *¡Suerte!*" He bravely accepted the challenge, muttering under his breath that it was no big deal and that he didn't know why I had made my experience the day prior seem so dramatic.

After about fifteen minutes in the bathroom with Broken Boy, Darwin came out with eyes wide and looking visibly shaken. He might have even turned a shade of green. He confessed, "I almost vomited and passed out. That was absolutely the worst experience of my entire life! This very afternoon we are going to buy him diapers. *No puedo volver a vivir esa experiencia.*"

I laughed wildly; he did not.

. . .

A few days later the electricity had been out all evening, and we had spent the last couple hours squinting in the darkness and shuffling around carefully, sharing the few flashlights we have.

Darwin and I then gathered with our five treasures in an official family meeting. We needed to figure a lot of things out. Together. I stood in the same clothes I had put on that morning before dawn, talking more than I should, the light of my headlamp helping the little red candle on our table shed sufficient light on our corner of the living room.

What started with frustrations and complaints from several ended with asking forgiveness and granting it. Then we all stood, joining our hands to form one body, and we gave thanks to God. We reminded ourselves that God's Word says that we must place *all* of our worries and stress in God's hands because He cares for us. And it is our task to believe Him and do so.

At the close of the prayer, I glanced at my husband and wearily asked the children to remember me in their prayers. My insomnia had been an exhausting roller coaster ride since high school. On many days I fought to fulfill even the most basic of duties and felt generally impotent due to such high levels of sleep deprivation. As newlyweds, my husband was alarmed by this often-unmentioned thorn in my side and took me to several local doctors, seeking second opinions and encouraging me to try numerous sleeping aids. After upping the dosages to potentially dangerous levels, still with no result, my husband, defeated, had all but given up and now accepted my condition as a crippling yet normal reality in our marriage.

Concluding the family meeting with my prayer request, Darwin and I then took each child individually into our embrace and reminded them how much we love them before everyone headed off to their sleeping quarters.

The following day as we zipped down the highway in our old pickup, spunky little Fireball leaned close and asked how I had slept the night before. Heavy rains beating down on our vehicle, she added, "All three of us girls prayed for you in our room last night."

I felt my heart sink into my chest, heavy with joy. Then Queen Bee, her elder sister by blood, chimed in, "*Sí; es verdad.* In our room we have a new system with Tender Heart of taking turns each night to pray for you so that God helps you sleep."

And with that the Lord granted me a deeper sense of rest than anything a good night's sleep can provide. He is teaching us to shoulder one another's burdens in love. He is knitting us, as different as we are and as uncomfortable and demanding as the process can be, into one body. *His body.*

Memorable Anecdote

Queen Bee to me, exasperated: "I'm frustrated because lately whenever there are problems with Broken Boy or conflicts between us girls, all you say is 'We're learning.'"

Me [laughing]: "Because we are!"

A Life-Changing Lunch

Spring 2012

Teresa took me out to lunch on my last day of Spring Break in Honduras. We had established a very open, direct line of communication during my stay, and we both felt it was important to ask each other all of our final questions before my departure. I ventured as we sat across the table from one another, "If I were to move here after graduation, what exactly do you envision me doing here?"

I hoped against hope that she wouldn't answer in such a way as to include me into the vast array of short-termers who plan to go somewhere for a season before moving on to their next great adventure. If I were to move to Honduras, I longed for it to be a permanent change in the landscape of my life, the beginning of many years of putting down roots and fulfilling God's call to mother and serve.

In her trademark, straight-forward, no-nonsense manner, Teresa chimed, "Well, you can see that I've been sick for many years, and I'm reaching a point that my health is just not letting me go on." I nodded.

Then she added, "I've been praying for many years that the Lord would send a younger person, someone to take the reins once I am no longer here. So, to answer your question, if you move here, I would train you for a year and then retire and return to the States."

We both knew she was not alluding to me taking over the music school; I couldn't tell the difference between *do, re,* and *mi* (although, thankfully, I could quite accurately distinguish a piano from a cello). What she *was* talking about was the children's home (a common synonym nowadays for orphanage), which I still was not entirely comfortable about participating in.

Excitement growing in my chest nonetheless, I clarified, "After the year of training, I would remain as the director of the children's home … *and be able to follow the Lord's direction in any way that He might lead?"* The direction I was convinced He wanted me to take was to transform that little children's home not into a distinguished institution that rejoiced in the big numbers and frequent short-term mission teams but rather into a small, intimate family, a hidden treasure of sorts where broken lives could heal quietly in the Lord's love.

Without missing a beat, Teresa confirmed, "Absolutely. I will share with you everything that I know during your first year here while you prepare to receive the first children. Then, you will begin the journey of raising the children in accordance with the direction God gives you." Against all logic, the seasoned woman across the table from me seemed utterly at peace with extending such a precious responsibility to someone so young. If she trusted God so unswervingly as to hand over her life's work to my care, I dared to trust Him in the same way. I felt the deep desire to live up to her high expectations and grow to fit the charge.

Leaning forward, fully engaged, I pressed one last point as my heart raced, "And I can be the mom? You recall that I shared with you the vision I believe the Lord gave me—"

She chuckled and shook her head good-naturedly, *"You can be the mom."* And that sealed the deal.

A Rescue Shop
Within a Yard of Hell

April 6, 2015

A small group of local youth have begun spending large chunks of time on our rural property, running around our yard and through our homes like wildebeests in rampage. Some are enrolled in our growing homeschool; others merely come to play. Almost all have this in common: Tía Tiki's active role in our town brought them to our front gate.

We do our best to tend to their needs and show them the love of Christ. We organize interactive games, arts and crafts, organic agricultural projects, and Bible studies. My husband includes them in his youth choir and teaches them the basics about musical instruments. Our efforts seem like a good starting point to expose them to healthy practices and a living hope for their future, but I still feel overwhelmed by the raw, gaping holes in these children's lives and development.

Many of these youth who now frequent our ranch have been left to virtually raise themselves as their parents assume little to no loving authority over them. Many of the adolescents are illiterate and have no working knowledge of simple math. Almost none have any concept of telling time or basic geography. Some have never been in school; others attend local public institutions but have learned virtually nothing.

We give hugs and talk about Jesus in the midst of our daily interactions with them, but the task of integrally healing, educating, and developing these young lives is so colossal that I honestly don't know where to begin. It's like trying to fill an Olympic-sized swimming pool with an eyedropper (while others are counter-productively scooping out the little water that you're accumulating on the pool's nearly dry floor.)

I have oftentimes asked myself, *Am I ready (and are our foster kids ready) to begin including so many other needy youths in our daily routines? Do I really have anything to offer these precious, yet wild children who come stampeding through our home nearly every day?*

We've recently become familiar with C.T. Studd's impressive quote, "Some want to live within the sound of church or chapel bell; I want to run a rescue shop, within a yard of Hell," and we sense that God is gradually transforming our ranch home into just that: a rescue shop within a yard of Hell.

To be honest, a rescue shop within a *hundred miles* of Hell sounds much more appealing to me, or better yet *within a yard of Heaven.* Oh, but the lost, broken youth are the ones we feel God has specifically chosen for us to love! This is our cross to bear.

Tía Tiki has indeed received these rogue local youth with open arms and has a special gift in loving them into the fold of Christ. For me it has proved much more of a struggle. Tía Tiki can oftentimes be found joyfully cooking with a group of children in our kitchen, Christian praise music blaring and the kids entranced by her warmth; I can be found trying to frantically shoo the children off the old couch in our common area that they've just jumped all over with their dirty feet. (Having visited our rowdy ranch a couple times, my dad refers quite accurately to this type of 'babysitting' as herding cats on steroids.)

Sometimes we have adequate time and energy to plan how to receive them *well* while on other days it seems like everything else has to be put on hold in order to be even peripherally present to the lives God has placed at our front gate. Sometimes there are triumphs or a breakthrough is made; other times the kids just lie and steal from us and make too much noise. Sometimes we *feel* compassionate; other times we just *are* out of obedience to our compassionate Father.

In this rescue shop within a yard of Hell, I feel as though perhaps I am rescued just as frequently if not more so than the lost boys and girls who wander up the long, isolated path to our ranch. My Father has stationed me at this post not only to catch those who might otherwise fall away, but to remind me daily of my own need of constant rescuing and forgiveness.

Memorable Anecdote

A hand-written note from 'Pa' Darwin to little Shadow Puppet:

I have seen you grow in so many ways, son. It is so good to see you so mature now; you sleep in your own bed without fear. You are such a big guy now; you no longer cry every time you take a shower. You are also doing much better at looking us in the eyes. You are our little champion. Remember that Ma Jennifer and I are here to support you in any way that we can because we love God and you.

The Best Gift:
A Home

Spring 2012

Upon finishing our brief, yet decisive, lunch, Teresa took me out
to the children's home's ranch property about half an hour outside
the city. We traveled by taxi, as she does not own a car. After
turning off the highway and traveling about a mile over a remote
gravel path, we came upon an extensive grassy property with a few
little empty houses in the distance. The rusty sign posted near the
front gate read *Rancho Hogar Agua Viva*, which in English roughly
translates as *Living Waters Ranch Home*.

Once inside the property's perimeter, the little old lady gave me the
grand tour of the project she had faithfully been investing in over
the past ten years. In awe, I thought, *I was eleven or twelve years old
when all of this started*. Teresa began with nothing more than a vision
she sensed from God and a deep desire to provide a loving home
for the trauma-stricken children of Honduras. Little by little over the
years, she, along with the help and initiative of several key churches
and individuals, had purchased the property and begun constructing
the buildings.

Taking in all that was around me, I was granted the privilege of
seeing the impressive result of years of dogged perseverance, faithful

generosity, and cross-cultural teamwork. The property was breathtaking and the buildings simple, yet functional. I followed closely on Teresa's heels as she meandered about the ranch.

As we stood on one of the little buildings' front porches, she looked up at me with a grin on her face and said, "This will be your home."

This will be my home. The Lord has given me a home! That short phrase — so loaded with meaning, as unbeknownst to her I had been crying out to God for months for a place to call home and put down roots — threatened to undo me right there.

Unaware of the incredible impact her short statement had on me, she smiled even bigger and suggested enthusiastically, "Can I take a picture of you?"

I laughed, suppressing tears of thanksgiving, and kindly denied her offer. This moment was far too sacred, and I felt too emotionally vulnerable for a simple snapshot.

There was not much else to see on the ranch, as the four cinder block buildings were practically void of furniture and other bells and whistles. The entire ranch could be compared to an empty, yet promising, shell. The only people to be found were the onsite watchman and his young wife.

Teresa and I soon left, both of our hearts full and marveling at how God had brought us together despite the odds (and despite my initial resistance). It had been a life-changing trip for both of us, and I needed to get back to the States to finish out my last couple months of university studies.

I would be seeing much more of Teresa in June — the timeframe we established for me to move to Honduras permanently and begin my year of intensive training under her experienced tutelage.

Low-Budget Horror Film

May 25, 2015

Broken Boy and Tender Heart, our newest treasures, have now enjoyed roughly four months of settling into our patchwork family. My husband and I consider that our daily follies may very well outnumber our triumphs, but we continue onward in the sincerest of parenting efforts. Broken Boy is slowly gaining more communication skills, albeit in his own special "language." Needless to say, all those who live in our household have likewise adopted his method of communication, which makes for some pretty hilarious conversations.

On this specific occasion, however, I wasn't thinking about our family's heartwarming evolution. My mind was drawn elsewhere.

Last night, I dyed my hair for the first time in my life, and it wasn't because I simply wanted a change of style. A gang in a nearby city had begun killing people with light brown hair, so people began dying their hair black to ensure that they wouldn't become the gang's next targets.

There I sat at the wooden table in our living room, everything illuminated by a few flickering candles because the electricity and water had been out all day, while a cheap cream was massaged into

my scalp to turn my virgin hair pitch black. My beauticians were
a twenty-two-year-old young woman, *already a mother of four*, and
a sixteen-year-old who was already "married," although neither she nor
her husband were employed, and she only completed the first grade.
Both young women had arrived at our gate with freshly dyed black
hair, kindly offering me their help. Seeing as we didn't have any
gloves, the elder of the two wore plastic bags on her hands, secured
in place with masking tape, so as not to stain herself with the potent
dye. It was a strange feeling, knowing I was the only one present
who could read the directions on the hair-color box *in Spanish.*

While I sat with a grocery bag on my head and dye creeping down
my sideburns, I opened up my Bible to share with them certain verses
that we had read as a family earlier that day. I spoke to my precious
beauticians of the injustice in our world that lies in stark contrast to
the perfect justice that so wonderfully characterizes our God.

In the middle of the whole ordeal, our preteen daughter, Tender
Heart, had an emotional breakdown, losing herself in the midst of
many obvious fears.

I squatted down in front of her and affectionately placed a hand
on her knee as I said, "There are so many things to fear in this
world — real things, scary things — that we can continually focus
on those things and feel perpetually paralyzed by fear, or we can
maintain our gaze on God, knowing that Jesus has overcome the
world. *Ésta es nuestra fe, hija.*"

I then looked around our humble living room with the collection of
family photos my husband Darwin and I had worked together that
morning to hang on a previously vacant wall. I reminded her of
that which we had already taught her on numerous occasions: "This
world is not our home, Tender Heart. Yes, I am at home right now
in the sense that I am in my own living room, and my children and
husband live here with me, but my real home is in God's Kingdom
with Him. *Este mundo no es nuestro hogar permanente.*"

I continued, the black dye hard at work making permanent changes under the plastic bag on my head, "God's Word says that the fear of God is the *beginning* of wisdom, and we learn that it is God's will for us that we don't fear other humans. So, if I fear the murderers and thieves and liars *instead of God*, I'm a fool. If I fear only God and, rather than fear the evil people or hate them, pray for them, I'm wise. So tonight, you and I can sit down together and pray for our own protection and the lives of those who are doing the killing, but we will *not* sit here paralyzed by the fear of man."

Towards the end of our long conversation in our dimly lit living room that evening, I embraced my precious daughter and reminded her once more: "There are two options: we can fear *only God*, and thus nothing else, or we can choose to ignore God and fear *everything else*."

In a matter of thirty-five minutes, my hair turned from a beautiful, completely natural, light brown to a tacky black with smudges of the stubborn hair color staining my ears, hairline, and neck. I looked like a pale witch cast for a low-budget horror film.

This morning as I rolled groggily out of bed and tested the light switch, still nothing happened. So, all the food in our refrigerator has now gone bad and I am left wearing a ball-cap that doesn't cover up all my hair nearly well enough, but God is good. My understanding of His goodness is renewed and strengthened every time it is put to the test, every time I am forced to choose between the two available fears: fear of the Lord or fear of men.

Memorable Anecdote

Queen Bee reflecting on the integration of Broken Boy into our family, who upon arriving opened the shower curtain while Queen Bee was showering and later snuck into her room and destroyed several of her personal belongings: "When Broken Boy came, I thought *I just can't put up with this kid*, but after getting to know him, he's stolen my heart."

At Ease, Soldier

Summer 2012

Elderly Teresa sat contentedly at her desk in the urban music school's empty living room, shuffling papers and organizing receipts. It was nighttime, and all the enthusiastic young musicians had left a couple hours ago, leaving the little yellow house in an abrupt silence.

I had graduated college a couple weeks previous and officially moved to Honduras shortly after. The bedroom that Teresa and I shared was attached to (or rather *inside*) the music school, as is a common practice here. Many hard-working people run a small business, art school, or ministry out of the same home where they live to save on rent and other expenses.

I eyed Teresa, anxious to converse, but likewise wanting to respect her space. I silently pulled up a chair. She took her gaze away from her papers to smile warmly at me. I ventured, "If you're willing — when you have time — I'd love to hear any advice you have for me. You have a whole lifetime of experience and have been here in Honduras fifteen years. I'm eager to learn from you, acquire wisdom."

With that, she stopped me and let out an unexpected belly laugh. I stared at her blankly, as I was not trying to crack a joke. She put up a small, wrinkled hand and said amiably, "At ease, soldier. We've got plenty of time for that. Go relax for now."

I protested, "But — I feel like I know nothing at all. When will you impart to me all that I need to know in order to live here and serve God effectively?"

She kept shaking her head and chuckling, "We already did a whole lot today. You'll learn as you go."

I got up from my seat, not entirely content with her instruction to "go relax," but intent on obeying. She added good-naturedly, "You make me nervous sometimes. You're like a little soldier, so eager to please. At ease; we'll be fine. You're doing great so far."

I, too, let out a chuckle as I thought she might be right; maybe I was too uptight and just needed to take things easy. She had, after all, used the "At ease, solder" line on me many times in the last few days, and maybe I needed to heed and learn the lesson.

Seeing Teresa's health rapidly and painfully decline before my eyes, however, I felt it became increasingly clear to me that we would not have a full year together as planned but rather much, much less. I felt desperate to learn as much as I could from her as quickly as possible, but she wasn't sharing much. In my youth and inexperience, I saw the older woman as a full, seasoned glass pitcher and me as a newly formed, small clay jar, ready and eager to be poured into.

But the pitcher wasn't pouring.

The Little Angel
in the White Dress

July 11, 2015

Recently, Tía Tiki and I arrived at a workshop for childcare workers held at a local hotel. "The experts have arrived!" beamed the middle-aged professional who would be leading the event, referring to the two of us. Tía Tiki turned to me to whisper playfully, "I sure could use the help of some experts!" And we both laughed, knowing how many times we've been in over our heads these last several months.

. . .

Two days ago, I found myself signing the now-familiar paperwork in the downtown office. We have accepted the challenge to love all over again.

Two of our girls had asked to come along with me for what promised to be a true "wild card" event. In the child protection agency's small bubblegum-pink building Tender Heart had gone to use the bathroom.

Queen Bee and I waited upon the arrival of the newest member of our family in the case worker's office. As I flipped through the (shockingly) thin manila folder that contained nothing more than a pending blood test and a one-page typed letter from the Honduran government legally placing the child under our custody, Tender Heart suddenly reappeared from her trip to the bathroom with somebody quite small connected to her right hand. Tender Heart looked close to tears as she told me that she happened across our new family member in the hallway.

Tender Heart looked sensitively joyful and gentle. I crouched before the little angel connected to her arm. We had been told she was seven years old, but looked to be more like five. (The agency later told us that no one knows her real age because she doesn't have a birth certificate.)

Before I could say anything, Tender Heart bent down and said to the little angel in the white dress, "*Ésta es mi mamá*," pointing up at me. "She will be your mom too."

I signed on the dotted line and we brought her home. The little angel now sleeps on a foam mattress on the floor in Darwin's and my bedroom until she settles in a bit. My husband and I sat on the cool tile next to her mattress and stroked her head and rubbed her feet as we sang to her about Jesus' love until she finally dozed off to sleep. Then we climbed into bed and listened over-attentive throughout the night at every little sigh, toss, turn, or cough.

You see, this angel has not known what it is to enjoy childlike innocence. Our little angel came to us with an unevenly shaved head that reveals more than a couple dozen raw bald spots on her scalp and a fragile body that has been cheated by malnourishment. Thus far in her life she had been used as her stepfather's sexual plaything; that is the only real information the child protective agency gave us. Her days have been painfully and humiliatingly marked in much the same way as those of a jaded prostitute.

Heightwise, *Chopping Block* doesn't even reach my belly button.

The first night little Chopping Block was in our home, Fireball, who had been with us almost two years, was saying things that a generally care-free child should say as all of us sat around together happily conversing in our living room. Fireball was explaining somewhat dramatically how her nose is the most sensitive part of her body, and if she bonks it on something, it will start to bleed.

Smiling and wanting to join in the conversation with her new family, Chopping Block perked up and shared in imperfect speech: "I's bleed from down dare," pointing to her vagina.

My body went cold. A mixture of paralyzing shock and deep compassion bubbled up within me as I stared at her, not knowing what to say. The room fell silent.

Yesterday, she, Broken Boy, and I were up early as I swung them back and forth on the two wooden swings hung from our porch. I whispered a prayer, asking God for strength and couldn't shake the notion that this would prove to be a grueling day after having slept only three hours that night and even less the night before.

"When's he comin' here? Am I's goin' back dare nest week?" Sitting on a porch swing, tiny Chopping Block blurted her questions out even as she failed to look at me directly.

I asked for clarity and quickly realized she was talking about her stepfather. I told her, a couple inches from her face, "He is definitely *not* coming here. What he did to you was not okay, Sweetheart, and I am so sorry about all you've been through. You can rest now because here he cannot touch you."

She began yelling about putting him in jail (exactly where that pervert needed to be), swinging past me back and forth on the front porch swing with increasing momentum. I gently said, "Chopping Block, I know you are mad at him, and I am too. I am *so* mad and heartbroken about what he did to you. Even so, it is my hope that

God will enable you to forgive him in time. Rather than hating him, we can pray for him."

Entirely unexpectedly, she put her short legs down to stop the violent back-and-forth movement, and looked at me and simply said, "Okay." She appeared expectant of something.

Caught off guard, I asked, "Okay … ? *Oh!* Do you want us to pray for him *right now*?"

That was, in fact, what she wanted, so I put my hand on her shoulder and began praying for the Lord to do a work both in her heart and in the life of the man who took what was not his.

About three minutes later, she asked to pray for him again.

So, our newest treasure holds my hand in tender moments at bedtime when every other waking second of the day seems like full-on warfare. Darwin and I stay up late praying for her and tell our new daughter about a Savior she can't see. We don't stop clinging to the belief in a God who can (and wants to) make all things new.

The Year that Turned into Eleven Days

Summer 2012

As the middle-aged driver and I helped elderly Teresa board the dark-blue minivan that would be driving her three hours to the airport, I sensed a deep impression was laid upon my heart that seemed to say, *You won't ever see her again.*

Since my decisive move to Honduras to live with the veteran missionary and learn under her tutelage, her already fragile health had begun spiraling downhill with alarming speed. Her nightly routine of countless prescription meds and self-administered injections had done little to help her carry on, and for the past several days she had been almost entirely bedridden.

Just a couple nights prior she had awoken around midnight and, on her way into the bathroom, slipped and fell. I had awoken and cautiously asked from the other side of the bathroom door if she needed help. I had seen my own grandparents' painful decline over the past decade and knew that losing strength and mobility was incredibly hard, especially for someone who prides themselves on being independent and capable.

From the other side of the door, Teresa had moaned painfully and affirmed that she needed assistance. I cracked the door open slowly as my heart leapt into my throat upon seeing Teresa in such a precarious position. She was on the floor in the small space between the toilet and the shower. I crouched down and began covering up her small, delicate frame with her robe that had gotten disheveled in the process. I cleaned her up and from there carried her back to her bed and propped her up at her request.

My heart racing, I wondered what I could possibly do to help her. She was, after all, my new boss, friend, and only real connection to the country of Honduras. I had long feared the possibility of her passing away or reaching a point of total incapacity, and I knew I had finally come to stare that fear directly in the face.

I sat at the foot of her bed and prayed silently. I then offered to give her a foot massage, and she gladly accepted. Her small, wrinkled feet resting in my lap, I lathered them with lotion and began giving Teresa an unhurried, soft foot massage. I asked if she would allow me to sing for her and she agreed.

With the small light of the bathroom barely illuminating our dark room, I sat there on the foot of my aged boss' bed and sang for her for several long minutes as my hands massaged her tiny feet. I have never believed that I have a particularly gifted voice for singing (and there have even been people who have not-so-politely told me the contrary), but I gave what little I had to offer over to the Lord and believed He was blessing my time with this hurting woman in the dusk of her days. I sang hymns and songs of praise, some of which Teresa knew and softly sang along to and others that she just listened to in contented silence. After a long time, she finally drifted off to sleep.

I silently accommodated her feet back on the bed and got up slowly, my heart still heavy from all that had just occurred. I turned off the bathroom light and slipped into the twin bed that had recently become mine along the room's back wall. I lay there, staring through the darkness at the ceiling, praying. Sleep didn't come for several more hours.

The next day, Teresa showed no improvement, and she finally made the difficult decision to return to the States for emergency medical treatment, as her degenerative disease had been exacerbated due to an onset of pneumonia.

I bid her farewell as she boarded that dark-blue minivan, with her promising through grimaces of pain that she would be back in a few weeks to continue the work she and I had begun.

I smiled back and gave her a warm hug as I stood in the gravel road in front of the yellow home that she and I shared. I held back tears as I waved goodbye. The minivan drove off, and with its disappearance around the corner I was suddenly cut adrift in a foreign land.

What was supposed to be a year together had turned into eleven short days.

The Real Chopping Block

July 21, 2015

A couple days ago I lay on that old floral print bed in our little town's local clinic receiving another IV. I spent several hours sweating profusely, as much from the blistering heat as from my fever that was breaking. I had brought a book along with me to read while receiving the treatment, but the Typhoid fever in my system caused great dizziness and fatigue, so my unopened book lay idly at my side.

Having arrived on the elderly Christian nurse's front doorstep many times in ill health, she has lovingly declared herself to be my Honduran mother, taking care of me in my times of greatest need and praying over me. My presence in her in-home clinic has become routine for both of us over the past many months, and we've formed a very special bond. This is just one area in which God has taken a difficult situation and transformed it into a blessing.

.   .   .

Recently, the very wiggly, shaved-headed Chopping Block lay on her mattress on our bedroom floor, my husband Darwin and I ready for her to go to sleep, but she was not yet convinced. I knelt down, cupped her sweaty, round little face in my hands (a technique I've begun using every time I want to get her full attention) and said in a high-pitched playful voice, wanting desperately to remind her how much we adore her even in the midst of so many daily disciplinary procedures and frustrating moments: "We are so content that you are here with us! *¡Te queremos tanto, chiquilla!*"

A smile immediately overtook her face, and she asked, "An' *Distance-Keepuh* too?"

Distance-Keeper is her older biological sister, who just arrived to live with us exactly one week after the first treasure did. As with Chopping Block, we don't know Distance-Keeper's exact age, but we are told she is between ten and eleven years old. The authorities had a hard time finding the elder sister because she spent her days wandering busy city streets collecting bottles, oftentimes until the wee hours of the morning.

To answer Chopping Block's question of whether or not we were happy to have her sister with us, I said, still holding her sweaty, less than pretty, scrunched-up face in my palms, "Yes! And Distance-Keeper too! *Las dos son tan preciosas*–"

Her response, interrupting me, "You's my momma, right?"

I chuckled, and, to answer the question that she has now asked 1,245 times, I said, "By God's grace, I am for now–" and was prepared to give a much longer explanation, but the stop clock on her attention span reached its limit, and she asked, "Now you's gonna pray foh me, right?"

After I stroked her feet and Darwin and I prayed for her, asking God's healing over her broken life, she sat up on the mattress, a large stuffed animal moose in her arms. (Earlier that day she had asked me what it was, and, not understanding what a "moose" is, she decided it was a sheep.) She demanded ecstatically, "Sing me dah music!"

At her request, Darwin and I began to sing songs of God's praise over her for about twenty minutes until she finally drifted off into a deep sleep.

Loving Chopping Block is not easy. It is not easy when she runs away from me at the bank or at the used clothing shop. It's not easy when she seems to have her own agenda on *everything* (and somehow, we didn't attend the same planning meeting). It's not easy when she takes things that aren't hers (and that sometimes are *mine*).

Yesterday our little popcorn kernel was disobeying as usual, turned her back on me, and began to scuttle across the front yard on a mission of her own when suddenly I heard a new kind of cry, a blood-curdling terrible noise. In over a week of knowing Chopping Block, I had yet to see her cry or show any form of weakness.

I hurriedly arrived where she was and bent down to her level. She looked up at me with huge crocodile tears in her eyes and the most awful expression on her face (it turned out she simply tripped and fell down), and I realized in the flash of the moment that *this* is the real Chopping Block. *This* — these terrible bone-chilling shrieks and contorted face — is probably how she spent much of her time in her previous life, being used as her stepfather's sexual plaything, enduring horrors that I cannot – *will not* – fathom. The little rebel, the sassy, loud-talking little girl who I had seen up until that point is some protective pseudo personality that has emerged, like bulky body armor with large, defensive spikes, to protect a heart (and body) that has been laid bare on the chopping block time and again.

Chopping Block and Distance-Keeper have other siblings who are still at large. On repeated occasions I have wondered why in God's mysterious providence He has rescued these two little girls off a large, sinking ship while several of the other passengers were not chosen. I numbly consider that we could (impossibly) take in 100 or 1,000 or even a million unwanted, mistreated children, and it would Never. Be. Enough.

Many a time I've wondered what grand difference being family to *seven* makes when there are so, so many more who need love and protection.

As hard as it may be for some to understand, I've come to the conclusion that at the end of it all, it's not even about the children. It's not about raising and restoring two children with tragic pasts, or thirteen, or none at all; *it's about God's glory, about light shining in the darkness.* As much as I love each of our treasures, I love them *because* I love my King, because my King loves them and has called me to do the same. It's not about taking kids off the streets and turning them into college graduates; it's about the Living God entering lives broken by sin and pain and calling them *home.* It's about believing that *one* life being touched with His love is as important to our Father as if a thousand were. Saving the world was never our job assignment anyway; it's God's.

So, I am coming (ever so slowly) to grips that if we only manage to raise these seven and never impact the hurting multitudes, I choose to believe that our assignment has not been in vain. I will fight to believe that Christ has overcome the world and has a sovereign plan. The world is in His hands, not mine. In the end, *He's* the Savior of the world, *not us,* and it's none of my business to worry about results anyway.

Reason Mocks

Summer 2012

With Teresa back in the United States to receive emergency medical treatment, I sat alone at the antique wooden desk in the bedroom she and I used to share. This room — *this house* — and everything in it was hers; I had only arrived on the scene a mere eleven days ago.

Her clothes hung in the closet; her toiletries sat on the bathroom sink; her impressive collection of books filled the bookcases. Her favorite foods sat chilling in the fridge and her personal agenda was splayed open next to her desktop computer. Her music teachers and her students streamed through her front door each day for classes under what used to be her direction.

As I sat alone in that eerily quiet one-story house considering my new reality in Teresa's home without her, I wondered what here — as much in this house as in this country — was *mine*. Perhaps nothing beyond the limited personal belongings that I had brought in my luggage less than two weeks prior. I had stepped into a virtual stranger's shoes, her life suddenly and irreparably thrust into my lap.

After considering my current situation in a somewhat detached, numbed manner, I did the only thing that seemed logical. I began calling my parents and friends to let them know what had happened. My mom was one of the first to answer.

She was understandably scared for me as she recalled hearing distant gunshots over the phone the last time we had spoken. She considered it obvious that without Teresa there was next to nothing for me to do in Honduras. Teresa had been, after all, the only delicate thread connecting me to this beautiful, turbulent nation. It was not my fault nor Teresa's that our planned year together got cut so drastically short.

From many others I received a similar and very well-intentioned sentiment: it was just too dangerous for me as a twenty-one-year-old foreigner (and female, at that) to stay in Honduras and walk the path before me without Teresa to lead and guide. It was time to come back home and rethink my future.

My chest tight and tears welling up in my eyes, I thanked each friend and loved one for their caring advice while thinking in despair, *But this is the home the Lord has given me.* I looked around me, suddenly remembering that nothing here was actually mine but rather Teresa's, and Reason seemed to mock me.

After having made the greater part of my phone calls, I brought my knees up to my chest and wrapped my arms tight around them, perhaps seeking solace. My head suddenly seemed to weigh three hundred pounds, and I let it fall forward slowly. There I sat in Teresa's old wooden desk chair with my head resting lifelessly on my knees for several moments.

Then, I was startled as the phone unexpectedly rang. I checked the caller ID.

It was one of the first people I had tried to call, but my attempts had gone to voicemail because the person had been busy. I sighed deeply. This next conversation would just be that one last straw to break whatever small measure of resolve I still possessed. I answered in a polite tone, my heart racing.

That Makes Eight

February 12, 2016

A few months ago, Tía Tiki moved to the city about a half hour away to begin working full-time with a local church. We are still in frequent contact with her, but we all miss seeing her on a daily basis after having lived alongside her roughly two years.

Yesterday evening I began to dish out dinner, mentally pushing to one side all I had learned from Tía Tiki.

When it comes to serving food in our home, you've got to be good at math.

Whenever the time comes to take out the cups, plates, and forks, you've got to do a quick mental headcount of who will be eating: some might be out at youth group (subtraction), while others might have invited friends over (addition). Serving food during daytime hours when all of our local students and small teaching staff are on our ranch can require knowledge of advanced algebra or calculus.

But last night, seeing as our kids, Darwin, and I were home together without anyone extra scheduled to attend, I put my mind on autopilot and began taking out nine of everything, which has been our magic number since Chopping Block and Distance-Keeper moved in several months ago. Seven kids plus two adults. (Hey, we're way outnumbered!)

As I began lining up all the plates on our kitchen counter, however, something felt odd. I counted the plates again. Yup, nine plates. Seven kids plus two adults, right? *Siete hijos*...

My mind groped in the dark, confused for a moment, until the still-very-new thought hit me: *No! Now there are eight kids! That's what was missing. Our new 'magic number' is ten.* I quickly added an additional plate, and suddenly everything seemed to make sense.

A couple months ago our preteen daughter, Tender Heart, who has now been in our family a full year, made a comment to me in a silly tone of voice. "If any new kids arrive in our family this next year, I sure hope they're younger than me."

Well, Tender Heart's wish didn't come true.

Last Thursday, one of our new students shared with us in prayer time the tragic reality of abuse she had been suffering at the hands of her stepfather for the past six years. The mother had gone to the police several times, filing official reports and pleading for help, but, as is frequently the case here, nothing had been done. As the story continued to unravel – taking on the horrific shape of so many others we've heard too many times – I felt a very strong prompting in my chest, and my husband confirmed the same.

We offered our precious, soft-spoken new student temporary refuge until her mom could escape the situation of abuse. The next day our student enthusiastically confirmed that her mom agreed, understanding our offer as being an answer to prayer.

Yesterday morning, fifteen-year-old *Team Player* came walking up our long gravel road in her school uniform to attend classes on our ranch. Our new treasure brought with her an additional grocery bag filled with all of her belongings.

What Could Have Been

Summer 2012

I sat scrunched up in Teresa's old wooden chair, bracing myself for my dad's opinion on my dire situation alone in Honduras.

My dad is a towering man with a 6'6" frame and years of athletic training under his belt. He studied at the Air Force Academy and has made a living as a pilot for one of the most successful international airlines. He is well-read and savvy with finances. He is, in many ways, the epitome of many of America's traditionally respected values and beliefs.

He is a strong, yet loving, man, but had difficulty comprehending my journey toward faith in Christ. A year or two ago he had expressed great doubts regarding the direction my life was taking, especially as I began making counter-cultural decisions and speaking of my desire to live a life of service to the poor.

I imagined faint-heartedly that he would have a field day with Teresa's departure. I felt I could already hear the I-told-you-so's that would be communicated over the phone. I waited, my stomach in knots.

He began, his volume markedly lower than I had predicted, "Jennifer, I am so sorry to hear about what has happened to Teresa. I can't imagine what both she and you are going through."

I froze, my guard suddenly demolished in one fell swoop. I confessed, now through hot tears, "Mom and everybody else have told me that I should return to the States, and I understand why they say it, but I don't feel peace. What do you think?"

My dad spoke in a slow, thoughtful tone I had never heard exit his mouth, "I am not a believer, but I know you are. I remember over Spring Break after you visited Teresa in Honduras you called me to tell me the decision that was made regarding your future. Your voice transmitted such assurance and joy about your plans that I believe you have to stay and at least give it a shot. I can't quote the Bible, but you say that God called you there. If you were to come home now, you'd never know what could have been."

Thick silence hung in the air for several moments; I think both of us were shocked at what he had said.

The Lord had used the unlikeliest of channels to speak His purposes into my life. Resolve burned anew within me. And, after one of the shortest but most pivotal phone conversations we ever had, my dad and I hung up.

I took out one of my disheveled notebooks and began intermittently praying and jotting down ideas for how I would take on this year of training in Teresa's absence. If she was no longer here, the Lord would doubtlessly teach and guide me using other channels just as He had affirmed my call through an unlikely one.

The Living Room Theology Class

February 29, 2016

Several of our older kids have begun giving our special needs children, Chopping Block and Broken Boy, tutoring sessions. The goal behind this is to help stimulate our two quirky ones who are the most developmentally behind schedule while granting our more mature children leadership opportunities.

This Saturday preadolescent Distance-Keeper (who is little Chopping Block's older biological sister) was the leader for the designated tutoring time. She has very short boyish hair that is just starting to grow out after having arrived at our front gate with all of it nearly buzzed off with huge bald patches, and she is very small for her age due to malnutrition suffered in her early childhood. She surprised me by taking the initiative to lean a large whiteboard against the wall in our living room and set up two wooden stools for her young squires. I sat on the floor in our bedroom organizing paperwork with our door open so that I, too, could sit in on what promised to be an interesting class.

Distance-Keeper, who just learned how to read, write, and do basic math for the first time in her life since moving in with us seven months ago, up until Saturday had not been one of our more dynamic tutors. She had generally been in charge of the "coloring book" tutoring sessions and, by what we could tell, had fulfilled her once-a-week class out of nothing more than a less-than-inspiring sense of duty to her little sister.

But on Saturday something had changed. This time she began enthusiastically writing the vowels on the whiteboard (which Chopping Block and Broken Boy have no idea how to read), and soon enough she had them sing-songing the letters of the alphabet in some catchy tune she had made up. The students were thoroughly engaged in the class, and she even had Chopping Block counting with her up to twenty.

Far exceeding the thirty-minute recommended time, Distance-Keeper dispatched her students to a short recess, telling me with a big grin that she wanted to keep teaching them other subjects even though she had already fulfilled her time commitment. She then informed me quite seriously, "The other tutors don't know how to manage Chopping Block and Broken Boy, *y por eso se comportan tan mal.* But I just tell them that if they don't listen up and participate, I'll take their recess away. That seems to work just fine."

I, too, took a short recess and crossed our front lawn, checking on the others and retrieving more folders for my organizational efforts from our little office building. When I crossed the threshold of our front door into our living room a few short minutes later, I was somewhat startled to witness that Distance-Keeper had already called her students in from recess and had them sitting obediently on their stools to continue the class. She was saying in a very even tone with more authority than perhaps I have ever heard her talk, and much less *teach*, "Of course we are going to die, because we are made of the dust of the earth." I blinked twice, frozen in the doorway.

Recovering from my initial shock, I passed quietly by them on my few-yards journey to our bedroom. I smiled at Distance-Keeper, intrigued, and she informed me matter-of-factly, "Now we're in Bible class." She had leapt from nursery rhymes to theology!

I nodded slowly, very interested to hear what Distance-Keeper-the-teacher (who did *not* have a Bible in hand) would be instructing her two very immature students on God's truth. I sat down cross-legged on the floor, this time with my mind much more focused on the theology class coming from our living room than on the manila folders in front of me.

She covered the beginning of Genesis with remarkable accuracy, instructing the little ones with all authority on themes that she has been learning in our weekly Bible studies but that, honestly, I had thought were beyond her. Of our eight children, she does not tend to have a lot of questions, comments, or prayer requests on any given occasion, and I had (very mistakenly) thought that perhaps she had not truly been paying attention. She had, however, come to give her life to Christ in one of our Bible studies a few months ago and we had seen distinct positive changes in her since then.

"God is love. He's the only true love we've got. The love of a person is small, but that of God is big — *más y más grande* — and He won't turn His back on you. Not even your mom loves you as much as He does. And if you repent, He'll be there. But if we don't repent, when we die, we'll be in front of God and He'll say, 'I don't know you.'"

After Distance-Keeper had instructed several times and in many different ways that God is love, Broken Boy started echoing her every time she said "God," him answering with an enthusiastic "A-moh!" (his way of saying "amor," which is "love" in Spanish.) And I think Broken Boy was onto something: every time we think about God, our knee-jerk reaction should be to meditate on His love.

She continued, changing the subject with surprising dexterity, "Now, Broken Boy, if I tell you to do whatever you want because you run your own life — like, go and have a lot of women — am I a good friend?"

Broken Boy, who wears diapers, answered shyly, "No."

Distance-Keeper: "*¿Verdad que no?* A good friend would tell you to submit to God's will and give away what you have to people who need it more than you do, and God will bless you."

She continued to teach as I jotted down her words from my nearby room. "Life is hard, even for children. A lot of kids can just run around and play all the time. But once you arrive in adulthood, things will be harder." She swung her gaze over to me to confirm, "Right, Jennifer?" I laughed.

"One day you two will be big, but you've got to start believing in God even now when you're small. You don't have to go around fighting — God says let there be peace and freedom, but no fights and wars."

Broken Boy started to giggle nervously, and Distance-Keeper corrected him. "We don't have to laugh at God's Word. This isn't like 'A, B, C' in first grade, Broken Boy — this is the true Word, and I'm not lying."

Broken Boy shaped up, and she continued, now teaching on the crucifixion, Lazarus, and the end of the world. "Not even the angels know when the end of the world will come, only God. *¿Verdad, Jennifer?*"

Her two pupils sat with total focus, listening to their young teacher who, by some miracle, already has God's Word stitched into her heart. She addressed her students, "Do you have a question about who God is?"

Chopping Block, stuttering and mispronouncing many words: "Dah— dah ... chaptuhs say dat we must love one anoder."

Distance-Keeper: "Very well, Chopping Block, but *first* we must love God."

"If I believe I am bigger than God, we are believing Satan, the father of lies. If I say I want to be the queen because God's dead, who's talking crazy? Me, right? Because I'm from the dust of the Earth, and God is the Father of truth."

At some point the class started winding down, and the teacher asked me what time it was. "2:20 p.m.," I answered.

She laughed out loud and said, "I think I'm gonna keep going until nighttime!"

Memorable Anecdote

After Chopping Block had received a stark behavior report from her special needs preschool teacher (in a class with only three other students) informing us that she had kicked and thrown herself on the teacher, eaten the other kids' snacks, lied, and screamed that she wouldn't be obeying anybody, Chopping Block came bounding through our front door the following day after class announcing triumphantly, "Ma! Jennifer! I's didn't kick dah teacher today!"

Have You Seen the Janitor?

Summer 2012

I was down on all fours, my hands and knees soaked to the bone and messily sliding all over the place. I had a dirty rag in my right hand and alternated between dipping it in a bucket of soapy water and scrubbing it over each square inch of the grimy tile floor. Sweat was cascading over my body thanks to the unspeakably hot, humid Honduran climate. As is common in many parts of the developing world, I was in a place without air-conditioning.

An older teacher poked her head into my empty classroom, sweeping her gaze in search of the new teacher on staff. When she saw that pitiful creature on her hands and knees in the back corner of the dim, dusty space, her eyes grew slightly in shock. Swiftly recovering, she said in a perky tone, "Oh, hi! I'm the third-grade teacher just down the hall. Have you seen the janitor?"

Janitor? No one had told me anything about a janitor! Where the heck was he, anyway? I dominated the urge to laugh aloud at the irony. If anything, it looked like *I* was the janitor on staff! I smiled at my new co-worker and answered politely, "Sorry, I haven't seen him." She nodded in a distracted manner and was off before I could introduce myself.

After my first few weeks of living alone in Teresa's melodious yellow house trying to manage her tiny non-profit music school with no musical knowledge whatsoever, I had made a few phone calls and began an official job search in the city. I would dedicate the year of what should have been spent in training with Teresa to training (and surviving financially) in a more hands-on fashion.

The director of the bilingual school enthusiastically brought me on staff due to my English-speaking ability and willingness to accept Honduran minimum wage, the equivalent of $350 per month for fulfilling a forty-hour workweek. Earlier that morning I was given the key to my classroom where I would be the urban school's only first grade teacher. The director assured me that I would be teaching no more than twelve to fifteen students, a manageable group for a first-time teacher with no teaching degree.

Everything in my empty classroom was covered in a thick layer of dust and grime, and I found more than a few scurrying cockroaches as I examined the obsolete contents of the small waist-high bookshelf in my room. There had been no training sessions for me and no manual to read; every time I asked to see the list of students who had enrolled in my grade, the kind-hearted elderly director assured me that they would give it to me on the first day of class. The school was a private bilingual institution that followed the American school calendar, so we would officially begin classes in mid-August, just five short days away.

During my evenings while overseeing the small music conservatory I Googled phrases such as "what a first grader needs to learn" and "first grader development." In essence, I was seeking a crash-course on how to effectively teach first grade. I found none.

I had no idea what I had gotten myself into. *Did first-graders already know the alphabet? Could they already write their name? Was finger-painting an appropriate first-grade activity, or was that more for kindergarteners? Help!* The more I Googled, the less certain I felt.

Nevertheless, the first day rolled around whether I was ready or not. I was clueless in regard to formulating lesson plans (and I felt I could not rely on the outdated, dusty American textbooks in my room, as my students would have no way of understanding them). My only preparation was that of a hand-scribbled note in my pocket with the only two activities I could think of: (1) every student would write their name on a slip of construction paper and decorate it, thus creating a fun name tag that we would then tape to their desk and (2) I would read the children storybooks as they sat in a circle attentively at my feet. The first day would be a half-day for all the students in the school. In my mind, my two planned activities were going to take up the four hours of classes.

I couldn't have been more wrong.

Dressed in my new school uniform, a collared button-down baby blue shirt with the school's logo and uncomfortable slacks, I felt like my heart was going to explode with joy as I bent down to individually greet each little person that came streaming through my door. I asked names, gave hugs, and met the parents. Everything was going along perfectly. After the fifteenth child walked in, I closed the door and began situating the children in their desks, ready to announce the first activity.

Then someone knocked on the door. I was startled slightly and went to see who needed me. I opened the door to see another tiny child standing there, looking up at me with big eyes. Number sixteen. The director had told me that I would have fifteen students maximum, but I supposed an exception could be made. I smiled sweetly at the little one and ushered her in, closing the door behind her.

Moments later, another knock. Number seventeen.

Then more tapping on the wooden door. Number eighteen.

The madness didn't stop until the twenty-eighth child entered my classroom. I felt frantic, like panic was clouding my vision. Twenty-eight wiggly students! I didn't have enough desks; the room was way too small; I hadn't been given any measure of supplies beyond the black dry-erase marker the school's overburdened secretary had handed me that morning.

Trying to keep my composure in the unbearably hot classroom, I smiled wide and informed my young students in their native tongue that I had a really fun activity for them to do. Only about five little girls were listening; the other twenty-three kids were busy climbing all over the desks, poking one another and talking way too loudly. I took out the construction paper that I had purchased with my own limited funds and tried to make the name tag activity sound more fun than it really was. My students each grabbed a slip of paper and jotted their name on it, taking all of about twenty seconds to finish the project that I had hoped would enthrall them for at least an hour.

No one was listening to me. *Oh, Lord. Be with me in my hour of need!*

Seeing that my first activity was a total bust, I grabbed the only few children's books off the shelf in my classroom — all in English, which the children barely understood — and invited them to sit around my feet in the back corner of the classroom, even though there was no longer space due to the excessive conglomeration of desks the director had to bring in last-minute. We pushed several of the desks aside to clear a small space on the tile floor, and I explained with as much love and authority as possible where I wanted them to sit.

Only a handful of my students obeyed me (or rather *heard* me) above the din, and even they lost interest in the book almost immediately as they couldn't understand the language it was written in.

Needless to say, those four hours of class my first official day as a teacher were some of the longest of my entire life. At 11:00 a.m., when the bell rang, I felt defeated and frazzled beyond my wildest dreams. Everything had gone haywire; my ability to control (and much less *teach*) my group of twenty-eight rowdy little ones was highly questionable. I couldn't imagine that what I had just endured was only a *half* day.

Starving and wanting to escape the school as quickly as possible, I packed up my things into my backpack and began walking home under the blistering sun. I passed by a small restaurant that serves delicious Honduran food and peered in. My stomach was roaring. I tried to order lunch, but the lady who worked there informed me apologetically, "I'm so sorry, Sweetie. We're closing. We only serve breakfast, and we're all out of food for today."

I felt on the verge of tears, not because of the lack of available food but due to the day I just survived — and the fact that I still had to go back four more days that week!

The woman sensed the desperation in my facial expression and posture. She promptly added, "Well, we do have two fried *pastelitos* that weren't sold at breakfast. Do you want them? It's all I have to offer."

Feeling as if I had been traveling aimlessly in the hostile desert for many days before an angel appeared out of the blue to serve me a glass of water, I couldn't have been more thrilled. I thanked her profusely before plopping down into a plastic chair near the counter. I buried my face in my hands while I waited, unaware that the waitress was still watching me.

When she approached moments later with the small dish she had promised, she probed, "Is it the heat, Sweetie?"

I stared at her blankly. *The heat?* My forehead still semi-resting in one of my hands, I answered "No, it's not the heat..." Then I blurted rather unprofessionally, "I pity my students! They have a terrible teacher! Today was the first day, and it was a total disaster. I'm not a real teacher..."

The waitress smiled knowingly and offered what encouragement she could. I swallowed the two fried *pastelitos* almost whole, paid, and then continued my short walk home.

That evening in the melodious abode I had come to treasure as home, I would be receiving one of my first beginner piano lessons with a middle-aged woman who had been a close friend and colleague of Teresa's. Before my piano lesson, I knew I had to think up a better plan for the next day of classes.

A Hospital for Souls

April 29, 2016

Recently a very well-meaning local friend of mine gave me a careful recommendation. She suggested that we do a preliminary selection process before accepting any new children into our family or school so as to hopefully eliminate those wily youth who just can't seem to get their act together, who are "too far gone," or who demand too much extra help and attention due to special needs.

Focus on those who can really succeed, those who really want to be "helped", my friend advised me.

To some extent and from a certain perspective, this thought can be rationalized and even embraced. Had we been losing our time with people who simply didn't want to be educated and parented?

The problem, however, is that when you run a hospital for souls, *everyone* who comes through the front gate is sick. Some are close to death and need intensive, prolonged treatment just to enjoy some level of stability (and even so they may *always* require their oxygen tank or weekly dialysis treatments), whereas others may stroll in with nothing more than a flu-bug or strep throat, receiving a quick, effective treatment so as to recuperate their vibrant health. Others arrive with chronic, degenerative illnesses. Others, mental health issues; some mere toothaches.

I cannot imagine a hospital where the doctors and nurses stand at the front door turning away the gravest of cases, receiving only those with ear infections, sprained ankles and skin rashes while refusing those with stomach cancer, blindness, and advanced diabetes.

This perspective is one that I believe the Lord has been teaching us during recent times (and not without much stubborn resistance on my part). I cannot tell you how many times I've been bewildered and frustrated to the bone with some of the cases that have walked through our front gate.

Oh, how easy it would be to just turn them away and accept only the cute ones, the obedient ones (if there even are such perfect children)! Yes, as weak humans we prefer those who only need a slight nudge in the right direction, a few safe prayers, and a reasonable investment of time, energy, and love in order to "recuperate" and enjoy the full life available to them in Christ Jesus. *Send us those, Father! The others are just too hard and require too much sacrifice.*

And yet every time we get ready to scratch one of them off our list and reach the conclusion that so-and-so is beyond all help, that quiet voice inside of us seems to say, *Don't be discouraged. Go to him and keep sowing the seeds of My Kingdom in his life. Hug her again. Grow not weary in well-doing.*

And so, we're learning how to persevere with the most difficult of cases even when we are tempted to give up. In the last several weeks my husband Darwin has made phone calls to families and reached out to boys who I had labeled "troublemakers." I've waded through nearly waist-high weedy overgrowth down abandoned paths, going door-to-door looking for the homes of our students who've gone MIA. I've sat on old couches to pray with discouraged moms and I've sat on moist planks of wood in our students' front yards seeking the Father's will alongside local families. We've made these search-and-rescue efforts a priority, and in the process I believe the Lord has begun re-shaping my heart to look a little bit more like His.

All the while, my ego — that huge, nasty beast that demands "easy" and "comfortable" and "*my* way" — is getting pounded into the ground one blow after another by the steady rhythms of God's love as He leads me from selfishness into self*less*ness.

Thus, many of the most difficult students that I secretly hoped would leave our ranch are still here, and we now thank God for this victory. This hospital for souls has not turned away the gravest of cases but is rather taking them on with great seriousness and love.

Yesterday evening my husband shook his head and said lightheartedly to me as I was preparing dinner, "If all these kids learn in their time with us is the transforming truth of God's love and nothing else, it's all worth it." All the music lessons, organized activities, and academic pursuits are good but are not the ultimate goal; loving and obeying God is.

I thank God that He doesn't give up as easily as I tend to.

Memorable Anecdote

One day as my husband, Darwin, and I crossed paths on our front lawn, he came over and gave me a peck on the cheek. Chopping Block saw us, although we thought nothing of it. As I headed over to greet Chopping Block moments later, she blurted: "Ain't dat right dat he's yo bofen?"

I am generally well-versed in her 'language' as her pronunciation of many words is catastrophically terrible, but in that instance, I didn't have a clue what she was saying. I asked: "What? What's 'bofen'?"

She pointed with an accusatory finger to where Darwin had walked off to, and said, "He's yo bofen."

I finally realized that she was saying her version of "boyfriend," and I laughed and said, "No, Chopping Block, he's my *husband,* that's like a 'bofen' for life."

Mystery Man's Phone Calls

Fall 2012

One month gave way to the next, and I continued to face each day in that downtown bilingual school where I wrangled my twenty-eight first graders. My first few months in that hot, cramped classroom proved to be grueling (and oftentimes embarrassing), but I grew to treasure my little ones dearly. And, with time and help from the school's more seasoned staff, I believe my students began learning.

Some of my sweetest memories with my students occurred each day after recess. Over time we had developed a special daily routine: each child would put their sweaty head down on their desk for several minutes while I would walk among the tightly-squeezed desks reading various passages in Spanish from my nearly worn-out Bible. I never felt confident speaking much English in the classroom, as they would always lose interest (and thus I would lose control of the classroom), but I have no doubt that the seeds of eternity were sown into the souls of each of my precious little ones. One afternoon one of my students' mothers, a local lawyer, approached me to say that that morning her chubby little son had commented to her over breakfast that "Miss Jennifer" had read the Bible with him and that he had learned that Jesus wanted him to love his enemies. That encouraged me, and I thought, *Maybe God is ensuring that something good will come out of my non-conventional teaching after all.*

An evening or two per week, Mystery Man would call the phone in the little music conservatory's main desk, which was located in the living room of the yellow home where I continued living. I had been in piano lessons a couple months and had even gotten involved in the small choir group while simultaneously trying to manage the administrative side of the music school in my free time each evening after teaching first grade. There were many balls in the air, and Mystery Man would call to see if the fort was being properly held down. The music conservatory, after all, was like his baby and had been home and mission to him for the past decade.

He was away in the United States studying English and music, but through our phone conversations he informed me that he would be returning to his native Honduras at the beginning of next year to take the reins of the music conservatory. Teresa's health continued to decline as she was shuttled in and out of emergency treatments and pain management programs in San Antonio. Mystery Man was concerned for Teresa, his long-time mentor, boss and friend, and he was likewise on alert to see how I was taking care of the music conservatory in both his and Teresa's absence.

With time I learned to recognize Mystery Man's phone number, as he was one of the only people who called me fairly regularly. His name was Darwin Canales, and although his photos were framed all over the yellow home where I lived, I had never met him personally. He was dark-skinned, clean-cut, and always seemed to be posing immaculately after a recital. The music professors and students spoke of him as if he were akin to a legend in these parts, and I never heard anyone utter a complaint in regard to his character. On the phone I would answer his questions — in Spanish — as best as I could, always ready to hang up after giving my official report of the music teachers' performance, payroll, student dropouts, and so forth.

Mystery Man would then cut me off politely, interjecting, "And how are *you*?"

I never expected that question, as my own wellbeing or otherwise surely was of no concern to him. We didn't even know each other!

Probing further, he would ask, "How did your morning go at the bilingual school?"

I would answer as succinctly as possible.

Again, he would probe further, showing uncommon levels of courtesy. And that's how the majority of our conversations went over the course of several months.

On my twenty-second birthday a couple months ago, alone in Honduras and still without any real network of friends, Teresa informed me from afar that Mystery Man had sent money to one of the school's music teachers so that they could buy me a birthday cake and celebrate. I was thankful for the thoughtful gesture and astounded at Mystery Man's unprompted kindness, although the birthday party itself was awkward and short-lived alongside party guests I barely knew.

Recently, I commented by phone to my mom about Mystery Man's inexplicably polite insistence in getting to know me, and she laughed knowingly, replying, "I think he's interested in you."

Triumphing Against the Blows of Fear

July 4, 2016

I paced in the little cottage we had rented during our three-year anniversary getaway; we were scheduled to head home thirty minutes ago. My husband Darwin had left nearly six hours earlier to go on what he told me would be a short walk. He hadn't taken his cellphone or wallet with him for fear of someone robbing it (he had been jumped not two months ago). My thoughts accused him for what seemed to me utter absent-mindedness. How could he have so lost track of time?

Restless, I sprawled out on the cottage's bed. I opened up my Bible to read, assuming that at any moment my husband would walk through the door all sweaty and happy after having found some remote stream or picturesque path by which he had spent hours. After all, two other days on our vacation trip he had left to go on a prayer walk and was away a couple hours, returning with a renewed mind and soaring spirit.

I love my husband's carefree, adventurous spirit, but this quality of his also has a knack for driving me crazy. I prayed a quick prayer — however odd it seemed and however put-off I was with his delayed arrival — that God would protect him if he were, in fact, in some kind of trouble.

About twenty minutes later a police vehicle arrived with Darwin in the backseat.

Darwin came hobbling through the gate of the small cottage complex, t-shirt drenched and ripped at the shoulder, several bloody wounds on his face and bruises on his arms. His tennis shoes were almost destroyed, one cheek swelled, black eye, and dark red marks around his wrists and neck. He could barely walk, but even so he flashed a boyish grin as he saw me. Surely, he wanted to appear fine to protect me so that I wouldn't panic. I wasn't so sure that his efforts were working.

The police escorted us to the local public hospital where Darwin shuffled into the emergency room and lay in noticeable pain on a bare table. I wondered groggily if they sanitized it between patients, as this public hospital is notorious for not having adequate supplies or even appropriate medicines on hand.

Lying face-up on the bare table, Darwin immediately recognized the emergency room nurse — an old classmate of his from college, I think — and they began to converse. She, as well as I and all others present, seemed to be thrown-off by his big smile and this-is-nothing attitude as his cheekbone and chin left a long trail of blood down his face and neck.

She stared at him in silent shock at first. My husband, after all, is known locally as a respectful, cultured musician who is passionate about helping children, not as a street fighter. She then asked the only thing that made sense: what could have possibly left him in such an unlikely state. He smiled and said, "Oh, I got kidnapped by a gang who thought I was someone else and they beat me up a bit. *¡Pero estoy bien!*"

Her eyes grew in shock as she asked empathetically, "But it was only for a few minutes, right?"

In the same upbeat tone, he managed, "Um, four hours." I sat a few yards away on a plastic chair that lined the wall, invisible, silent, and pale.

Throughout the hospital visit, two police officers and a local friend of ours kindly accompanied us. Taking turns, we constantly swatted away pesky flies that wanted to land all over Darwin's open wounds.

I studied the two police officers, one in his early twenties and the other a pot-bellied, middle-aged man. They were both fully armed and decked out in their bright-blue police uniforms. They stood poised and ready to lend a helping hand, perfect gentlemen. They were in no rush to leave us alone in the hospital, and you could see in their expression that they were genuinely sorry about what had happened to my husband.

I politely commented to the older police officer, "Thank you so much for all you've both done to bring my husband and me here to the hospital, but please go now and try to find the men who did this to him. Justice must be served speedily before they go into hiding. My husband can tell you their location, and I'm sure he could easily identify who the men were if he is shown photos of the suspects. *Por favor, apúrense."*

The police officer shook his head disappointedly, lips pursed, and muttered some excuse that lacked logic. There was no sense of urgency about him or his partner, and after a moment's pause he commented matter-of-factly that he already knew there was a severe gang problem in that neighborhood. Recently there had been many other cases of violent abuse coming from the same area.

I stared between them both, a confusing brand of rage gaining momentum within me, as I thought, *They have no intention of actually going after the men who attacked my husband. Their idea of "justice" is accompanying victims to the hospital!*

Another young man with similar fight-wounds and open gashes sat unaccompanied on the table next to Darwin's. I couldn't help glancing between the two of them. Was this other young man — much closer to his teens than my husband — a gang member who sought out a fight and lost, or is he another innocent, honorable citizen who fell prey to terrible abuse?

I would never know because I certainly wasn't about to ask.

X-Rays, shots, stitches on my husband's cheekbone and chin. Buy pills, push him around in a wheelchair to different rooms of the hospital. Take his shirt off and find his entire back marked in a deep, dark purple. Distinct shoe-print bruises all over his back, open gash on his leg that wasn't previously visible due to his attire.

Darwin's adrenaline and will to cover up his suffering was running out; his body began to tremble. Mine continued on in a very hollowed numbness, accompanying him in ghost-like fashion to and fro within the rundown public hospital complex.

Through very slowed thoughts (made much worse by my insomnia the night prior), I somberly confronted what I've known since the day I married Darwin three years and one day ago: at any moment he — or I — may get killed. A long marriage — a long life — in this nation torn by violence and sickness is no guarantee.

I did not cry, did not scream, did not become paranoid, did not question why God allowed this to happen. Merely, I understood that this always *could* have happened and still *can* happen again. Death is always close. In any country, any place.

As one hour in the hospital turned into two, I learned more of the story: Darwin had been walking off the beaten path — as is his terrible habit — when a group of four young men crossed his path, all of whom are involved in a gang that makes its living off of extortion and murder. They found it suspicious that a man would be wandering down along a stream all alone on their "territory." Seeing it necessary to interrogate him to see who he worked for and why he had been sent, they forcefully took him to a nearby neighborhood, the zone they control.

What ensued were the longest four hours of my husband's life. There were many innocent passersby who witnessed the process of interrogation and torture in broad daylight on a public street. The gang leaders falsely cried out, "He's a thief! *¡Es un ladrón!* He deserves this!" Everyone, controlled by fear, just kept walking and looked the other way.

The group swelled to seven men. They promised to cut his ears off; they promised to kill him. His solemn response even as he bled in the dirt: "If it is God's time to take me, then I'm ready."

They shrieked at his responses, mocking him for his "Christian" claims. They howled, "Surely the Christians wear suits and ties, not shorts and tennis shoes! *¡Qué mentiroso!* He's not a Christian! Hit him harder until he confesses what gang he works for!"

After four hours of intense physical torture and violent bullying, they spared his life without any apparent reason. Perhaps it was because he did not cling to it too tightly.

He stumbled away as he took a back-route through a mountain stream, zigzagging across pineapple fields and then eventually arriving at the highway where he found the police station, collapsing upon arrival.

As he lay on the hospital table, I sat near him, still feeling like a ghost. He whispered something to me that put everything in perspective. "Just imagine, *amor*, they were so scared. That's why they did all that to me. Fear is what drives them."

Yes, *scared*. Not my husband, but rather those who tortured him.

A normal person would respond, "What? *They* were scared? How is that? Don't you mean that *Darwin* was scared?"

No; those men, perhaps evil personified, went to the extent they did because they feared Darwin was from an opposing gang. Fear controlled them while Darwin, receiving the physical blows, received no blow to his peace, for it is not found in nor based on what happens in this world.

We were at the hospital for several hours, and the two police officers silently, but compassionately, accompanied us throughout the process. They never asked Darwin any questions that might be pertinent to an investigation; they didn't write out an official report or even ask his full name. They helped me push his wheelchair and stood patiently in each exam room with us. Had they been normal citizens, I would have thanked them effusively for their exemplary sacrifice in accompanying us in our hour of need. Being agents of justice (and effectively denying their role), however, only deepened the bloody wound of confusion and rage within me. I found their presence among us to be a cruel mocking of my husband's unjust suffering, and with each passing hour I couldn't help but numbly consider that any hope of justice was slipping away forever.

That evening we arrived home from the hospital to be greeted by highly concerned kids and a household that needed to be put back in order. Darwin sat uncomfortably hunched over on a small wicker stool in our living room and told the story to our older girls (at their request). All of them sat on the floor in front of him. I sat in their midst.

Cloaked in an utter transparency — and not in some hyper-fear or story-telling exaggeration — he told them calmly of both the physical events of the day and their spiritual implications. He truly felt close to Christ, came to understand even a little bit more the unjust sufferings of our Savior at the hands of evil men.

Our treasures sat cross-legged at his feet, tears welling up in their eyes at the thought of having almost lost the only loving (human) father several of them have ever known. Preteen Distance-Keeper sat on the floor a few yards removed on the other side of the door-curtain in her room, wanting to hear but not wanting to see.

As Darwin finished, I carefully added, fully convinced of my own words, "We should give thanks to God even for this; the Bible says we are to give Him thanks *en todo momento*, both in difficulties and in times of ease." As my heavy statement fell on young, scared ears, Tender Heart's eyes grew, and her head shook back and forth in protest.

I could read her thoughts: *No! I will not give thanks to God for this.* I tilted my head to one side as my eyes gently met hers, and I prayed that someday she might understand this aspect of biblical wisdom.

After a long evening, I went to preteen Fireball's top bunk to kiss her good night. With a big smile she showed me a white piece of paper taped to the wall next to her bed marked with her scribbly writing: "Goals for Fireball to fulfill."

My eyes passed over her sloppy cursive handwriting as I came upon her second goal: *I will give thanks to God for everything, in difficulties or trials or good things.*

My heart swelled with gratitude as I read each of the goals written in large print. She studied my face and then told me, "This afternoon when you said we should give thanks to God even for what happened to my Pa, I thought you were wrong. But then this evening I feel like God revealed to me that that is, in fact, what we should do. We should *always* give Him thanks, even when bad things happen!"

A few minutes later I finally collapsed in bed next to Darwin, where he had spent the evening in the fetal position. Exhausted to the bone, but without the least onset of sleepiness, I took my Bible out and wedged our flashlight between my shoulder and ear to illuminate the page in the otherwise dark room.

Several moments passed before Darwin asked in a strained whisper, "What are you reading?" Feeling as though that simple question had just come from the mouth of a dead man, I let the flashlight travel up the wall in front of us above our bathroom door, shedding light on the simple black sticker-letters that we placed there so many months ago that state the biblical truth: "He takes care of us." Neither one of us said anything as we let our eyes trace and then retrace the words.

Then, unexpectedly, a little collection of folded papers slid under our door, a *swoosh* audibly heard on the tile floor in the silence of the night. I got up to retrieve them. They were from Fireball. She had prepared several love notes for her Pa along with a rather long and thoughtful list of Bible verses she wanted to encourage us with.

Minutes turned to hours and Darwin had long since fallen asleep; I wandered into our little cave-like bathroom and sat. Still no tears, no overwhelming fear, no questioning. As I sat on the closed toilet lid with my head resting in my hands, a new revelation — so simple, so obvious — dawned upon my heart:

Life is incredibly simple. There are two opposing forces: God, Father of life and truth, the good King of the coming Kingdom, and Satan, father of lies and death, prince of this fallen world. As this very real battle rages on in this world, we are given the simple instruction to love: to love God with all that we have and all that we are, and to love one another as we love ourselves. God takes care of the rest; through Jesus we triumph with God in the end. Too often we run around, worried about our jobs and reputations and travels and our own desires, complicating -- and possibly missing altogether -- what is actually shockingly simple.

Now, nine days later, Darwin's physical body is almost completely healed, and I'm clinging to that fading revelation that God granted me alone in our bathroom during that midnight hour. In the midst of long days and nearly no-sleep nights, I plead to God for such clarity as He had granted us on the day when Darwin's life was nearly taken.

In this world we will have trouble, but we must take heart, for Christ has overcome the world.

Memorable Anecdote

A love letter from Tender Heart to her 'Pa' Darwin:

You are the dad I never had. Now I have someone to give Father's Day cards to. Now I have you, Pa. I will give you all my time that you need; if you are sick, I will take care of you and help you get better. You no longer have to pay to go to the local clinic; my pay will be your smile. Even if my biological mom comes to get me someday, you will always be in my heart. You'll always be the dad I never had.

The Problem Is, They're Still Orphans

Fall 2012

Throughout my first several months living in Honduras, I dedicated a good portion of my weekends to traveling on rundown public buses to visit local children's homes and orphanages to learn from those who've dedicated their lives to orphan care. I considered this an important part of my hands-on training for the future work I would be doing, and I was thankful for the many directors who graciously opened up their homes to me and generously answered my many questions.

I discovered that some homes raised only boys; others only girls; others mixed. Some had a rotating staff; others had more permanent "aunt" figures who took care of the children. Some were even privileged to have "uncles" on staff who served as stable, loving male role models. I learned that most homes preferred receiving small children; experience had proven older kids and teenagers to be too risky. The vast majority received a constant flow of foreign visitors and short-term mission groups; I could sense that many of the children knew that whoever walked through the front gate most likely wouldn't be in their lives for longer than a week or two. Most of the homes' directors lived apart from the orphans in their own private quarters where they dedicated a good portion of their time to raising their own biological children.

Without fail, in each home, I was impressed and inspired by the directors' and staff's selfless service and loving attitudes toward the many children under their care. In almost every home, however, I noticed a heart-breaking reality: the children entered as orphans and when they left, sometimes even after spending many years in "the system", *they were still orphans.*

And what's worse, the kids knew it.

Is it not God's vision to scoop up the orphan in His mighty palms, transforming him or her into a beloved son or a treasured daughter? Surely, we do not come to the Lord only to continue as lost, orphaned souls in the world; no, the Bible says He *adopts* us, and we become His beloved sons and daughters for all eternity.

As I visited one institution after the next, I could not help but feel that the children who had a half dozen caretakers did not truly have parents. Aunts came and went; some were fired; others got married and moved on after a season of exhausting service. I sensed that the children in most of the homes I visited (but not all) knew deep down that there wasn't even one responsible, caring adult to whom they were permanently tethered. The staff's commitments and short-term visitors' agendas were constantly shifting around them; they knew that many good-hearted people would enter their lives to give them gifts, maybe lead a vacation Bible school for a week, and then eventually leave. They knew they had entered the home as orphans and at age eighteen when they left, they would most likely leave under the same devastating status.

This utterly and irreparably broke my heart, and one day as I squeezed into a broken back seat on a hot public bus, I prayed fervently that the Lord might enable us to do things differently. I still had no idea who would stand beside me day after day in the work that lied ahead, but I sensed the Lord would send the right people in His timing and that He would give us a different vision for orphan care: *family.*

May the children You send us come to recognize themselves first and foremost as Your beloved sons and daughters, but also as ours. Just as I believe You've promised me a home within Your perfect will, I ask the same for my future children. Bring them home, Lord.

One of God's Slow Miracles

July 11, 2016

This past Saturday was little Chopping Block's one-year anniversary since moving into our home.

Although her annual landmark was written in large print on our family calendar, the day came and went without much hoopla. In years past we celebrated not every *year* but every *month* a child was with us, for everything was so new and so difficult that each day survived was an incredible triumph. Now, however, with a bustling household of eight precious treasures and even more students and local teaching staff, all of whom have countless special dates to be remembered, the celebrations are becoming less extravagant. Our days have become more planned and less spontaneous. Adventure has given way to routine, and many of the warm-fuzzies are long gone.

So, on Chopping Block's one-year anniversary as she and I walked hand-in-hand out to Dingo's pen to fill up his dog bowl together, the Lord utilized that small timeframe to open my mind beyond the daily, the immediate. Memories of an entire year spent with Chopping Block flooded over me, and I received each one with heavy-laden gratitude, battle-scarred joy.

Chopping Block, whom one year ago I had met for the first time, that little angel in the white dress with the unevenly shaved head. Chopping Block, a mere babe who'd undergone more than many adult women do in a lifetime.

Chopping Block, who months after having moved in began to shed the first of many layers of pain and anger, leaving her an empty shell, a little ghost. All she had known was rape, sexual games, abuse, neglect. So, you take all that away, and what was left? She was our hollow little girl who we desperately wanted to fill with the Father's love.

And, in many ways, she still is.

Her psychologist informed me just a few days ago that she has made many strides and is mentally *now* on the level of the average three-year-old. *And before?*

So, she and I walked this past Saturday, hand-in-hand as we always do, as she eagerly offered to help me fill up Dingo's dog bowl. She loves to help me. I appear to be her favorite person, after all, which is an incredibly demanding blessing. She's made great strides to overcome malnutrition and now physically looks to be nine or ten years old but still has the intense emotional needs of a toddler. Daily I cradle her heavy body as you would a baby, kiss her sweaty forehead and nose, bounce her on my knees.

And it's never enough. She constantly wants to be in my arms, under my skin, in my womb.

As we're hugging each other or as I'm cradling her, she'll often look me in the eyes and whimper, "I's missin' you, Ma."

I want to cry to the heavens, "How can she miss me? I'm right here! *¡No puedo estar más cerca!* Oh, Father, fill up this little one because I simply cannot! Fill her with Your love!"

Crossing our grassy front yard together on Saturday, I wearily contemplated the utter fullness of this past year with her in all of our ups and downs, all our little triumphs that when marked on paper or pronounced aloud seem like nothing at all. In my heart I asked God what He thought about all this, about Chopping Block.

After all, I've considered the world's answer and my own quite a few times and, honestly, it's not very encouraging. She may never fully recuperate, may end up struggling onward well into adolescence and adulthood with promiscuous sexual tendencies, theft and mental retardation. She may never learn to talk correctly, may present these incredibly intense emotional needs for many years to come without any apparent improvement. She's a heavy load that no one can carry. In short, we very well might be wasting our time.

Chopping Block and I were nearing Dingo's pen. Not a moment after having asked God what He thought of our broken little angel and the work we are doing of raising her, I felt He sliced through my whirlwind of woes with this piercing question: *Are you loving her, and are you teaching her to love Me?*

Borne somewhere in the deepest recesses of my inner being — overcoming the daily exhaustion and general discouragement like a powerful wind — a peace blew over every corner of my soul. My busy thoughts were immediately settled as I recognized the truth: *Yes, we are.*

We had reached Dingo's pen in a few short moments that to me had expanded into eternity. Chopping Block was chattering on about this and that, always with her stubby little hand firmly grasped in mine, but her voice somehow didn't reach my ears. What I felt I heard, my inner being completely stilled, was this: *Then all that is being done with and for Chopping Block is a success. The purpose of the entire universe is to love Me with all that you are and to love one another as yourselves. If you are doing that and teaching Chopping Block to do the same, you are fulfilling the one and only purpose I have set for mankind to fulfill. Nothing else matters.*

God forgives us by Christ's blood and now calls us to love — not to change the world, invent something new, or reach great heights of human "success." In all of our imperfect efforts of loving, failing, seeking forgiveness, and trying to love again, He is pleased. If Chopping Block never learns to assimilate into normal, productive adult society; if she's always a step (or a thousand steps) behind, but is being shown God's love and being taught to love Him in return, her life will be a raging success in His eyes even as the world mocks, demands more impressive results.

Our journey with Chopping Block is one of God's slow miracles, etched out over time, heavy with the promise of great eternal rewards. And, when I am tempted to become impatient, to want to push her hard and fast toward normality, I ask that God might remind me of what He taught me just two days ago out at Dingo's pen with Chopping Block's stubby hand in mine:

As long as we are wrapped up in the divine task of loving in Jesus' name, we are fulfilling the ultimate goal for the entire universe. Nothing else matters.

She Just Doesn't Know It Yet

Winter 2012

At the end of his time abroad, Mystery Man packed up the few
belongings he had and bid his warm farewells to his professors and
classmates. He had been studying at an international university in
San Antonio, Texas — the same city I grew up in and where elderly
Teresa had been taken for emergency medical care several months
prior. He was one of the older students in the university group,
but his charisma and easygoing personality helped him make friends
wherever he was.

He had recently sung in Teresa's funeral at a local church, which
had been the solemn closing of a life-changing chapter in his life.
She had taught him the foundation of all he knew about music
and had led him to the Lord. And, transcending typical professional
bonds, they had provided one another kindred friendship in
increasing measure as her health declined over the years.

Mystery Man held within him the intent of returning to Honduras
to take the reins of the little music conservatory that Teresa had
left behind. Years ago, he had earned his college business degree on
Honduran soil and had been prepped to eventually take over the
director's role of the music school where he had worked so many

years under Teresa's tutelage. His uncommon level of selflessness paired with his passionate tenacity to teach made him perhaps one of the only true candidates for the role. His years of experience toiling alongside Teresa in their struggling little non-profit music school had reaped him little to no financial dividend; he was all-in not for personal gain but rather to serve.

That kind of person can be hard to find in any country.

What Mystery Man's university comrades in Texas didn't suspect was that he secretly held other motives.

He approached one of his favorite English-as-a-second-language professors, a middle-aged woman, in her pristine, air-conditioned classroom. When he bid her farewell before departing for Honduras, she probed him, "Why so soon, Darwin? We all thought you would be staying for another semester or two." After all, who in their right mind would hurry up to return to their struggling third world country when given an open invitation to learn and grow in a more prosperous nation?

He smiled from ear to ear and answered, "I'm returning to Honduras to get married."

The professor stared at him in a momentarily silent state of shock, as Mystery Man had been the epitome of the content single man throughout his twenties. He had been active in church groups, highly dedicated in his work, and extremely respectful around the women in his life. He wasn't known for flirting with anyone, and he was the polar opposite of the stereotypical serial dater. Several people had even tried to set him up with cute girls over the years, but none of them seemed to be quite what he was looking for. *Darwin was really going to get married? No one even knew he had a girlfriend, much less a fiancé!*

Well, he didn't.

The professor sputtered in a motherly tone, "Oh my, congratulations! Who is the lucky girl?"

His contagious grin stretching even further, he answered with a sparkle in his eyes, "Oh, she's already in Honduras. We're going to get married soon. She just doesn't know it yet."

And with that determination he returned to Honduran soil, ready to put down roots of his own.

Compassion Shown by the Unlikely

September 19, 2016

On Friday in the early evening, I was in the midst of applying antifungal creams, encouraging young readers and commanding small soldiers to pick up scattered Legos. I glanced at the clock — barely 7:00 p.m. — and sighed deeply as I wondered where I would find the strength to continue in the daily bustle. Living in a state of almost constant sleep-deprivation is more than I can gracefully bear.

Suddenly, preteen Distance-Keeper intercepted me. She stood up from where she was playing piano and very intentionally put herself in my path. It was clear she intended to add to my to-do list.

With her small, beautiful, round face illuminated with joy, she asked, "Can I talk to you?"

That simple phrase often indicates the beginning of a long, sit-and-pour-your-heart-out conversation that can potentially last a very long time. In the evening after a long day is not my finest hour for such a chat.

My morale immediately dropped (and probably my face as well) as I imagined I would be spending a good chunk of time — and a good chunk of emotional energy that I already didn't have — listening to my undersized daughter.

I answered wearily, hoping against hope that it might be something quick like Can-you-give-me-the-hydrogen-peroxide-to-pour-on-the-scrape-on-my-knee, "Ok, go ahead. What is it?"

She answered with equaled (or perhaps increasing) joy, undeterred by my unenthusiastic response. "No, not here! *En privado*."

"Oh … okay." *Dang it.* "Where?" *Not in private!* That indicates a longer, more intense conversation! *Lord, I have nothing left to give. Please accompany me in this moment and give me the grace I need to listen to whatever she may tell me. I'm so tired.*

She smiled and indicated for me to follow her into the bedroom she shares with her little biological sister. Wooden bunkbed with mismatched, but clean, bedding. Big plastic bucket as clothes hamper. An unclothed baby doll and a stuffed tabby cat toy on the bottom bunk. Wooden dresser shared by both. Antique (as in, very old) wooden chair with a fading blue cushion. Floor impeccably clean — swept and mopped to perfection — and all belongings in their place after having spent the morning cleaning together as a family.

I remained close to the doorway, my body language communicating my heart's hidden intention: a quick escape if things got hairy.

Distance-Keeper began in an upbeat tone, very frank yet respectful, catching me off guard with her directness, "You're in a bad mood, right? *La veo un poco estresada*."

My heart sank. *Oh no. She could tell I was frustrated. Great self-control, Jennifer. Did I really look that bad?*

I mustered a sincere smile and answered, carefully managing my tone of voice, "No, I'm not in a bad mood, Sweetheart. I'm just really

tired. But I'm okay; that was very kind of you to ask." My body
turned slightly toward the doorway; I was ready to leave.

Her facial expression indicated that she anticipated I would answer
that way, so she threw up her thin, muscular brown arms with clear,
innocent eyes and asked, "Can I pray for you?"

That was why she had asked to talk to me in private. She had
taken note of my fatigue and intended to pray for me.

Just the day prior this young woman and I had experienced a heated
conflict which was ultimately resolved in both parties asking for
forgiveness and granting it. The intense battle came to a close as she
had sat in her antique armchair and I had prayed for her.

So then, the day after our timely reconciliation, she stood before me
asking if she could pray for me. I felt as though I could not answer,
had not rehearsed for this. Prayer is a normal part of our daily life
together – but *her* taking the initiative to pray for *me*? This little
treasure making the effort to search me out, chase me down with
love when she saw I needed encouragement? None of our kids had
ever done that before.

Sensing my surprise, she shrugged, eyes still very bright, and
informed me with total assurance, "I feel that it's what God wants
me to do." I nodded awkwardly, words still escaping me, and I took
a few strange steps toward that same antique armchair that marked
our reconciliation from the day prior.

I sat down, still unsure how this would go and at the same time
feeling incredibly blessed by this little one's faith flushed out in
deeds in the midst of what was one of my less inspiring moments.

She instinctively squatted down in front of me — the posture I take
with our kids many, many times each day as a way of getting on
eye level with them (especially because I am extremely tall) — and

reached for my hands that rested idly in my lap. Our posture — me in the chair, her squatting down, embracing my hands — was a perfect reversal from the day prior.

She immediately bowed her head and began praying for me out loud with great confidence, admirable faith. She asked God to grant Darwin and me the perseverance to continue onward during many years to come. She prayed that I may be granted rest, that even in difficulties God would grant me great joy.

Having reversed roles, if only for a moment, this small preteen had been used by Father God to express compassion and faith to this discouraged mom.

Feeling blessed after having received such undeserved compassion from an unlikely person, I stood up and gave her a big, slightly awkward hug. My tall frame enveloped her small one as her face disappeared somewhere in the middle of my torso.

I re-entered our living room and noticed through the boys' doorway that Broken Boy was already lying in his bottom bunk. With renewed faith, I asked if I could come in. His response was an enthusiastic "Sheah, Ma! Sheah!" slightly dulled by sleepiness.

Whereas on most nights it's a quick good-night-hug and kiss-on-the-top-of-the-head and off-to-bed-you-go, Distance-Keeper's daring act of faith inspired me to step out of the boat as well, to take up my cross and joyfully follow Christ even when it isn't easy. I bowed my head — Broken Boy's eyes squinted intensely shut as his whole face crinkled up in prayer, my fingers tracing up and down his baby-soft arms — and I prayed for Broken Boy, daring to ask God to heal this sweet little boy even as He heals me.

Mystery Man
in Person

Winter 2012 — Spring 2013

My first December living in Honduras I returned to my Texas roots
to spend the holidays visiting family and friends. While I was away,
Mystery Man had returned to Honduras. In essence, we had switched
locations. He was joyfully back in his native land and had diligently
begun putting everything in order at that little yellow melodious
abode I had come to call home.

A couple weeks later and back on Honduran soil to begin my
second semester teaching my rowdy first-graders, I got out of
a taxi in the pouring rain with the little luggage I had taken
with me. As I approached the music conservatory's front porch, my
attire completely soaked, Mystery Man opened the front door and
chivalrously took care of my luggage before I even knew what was
happening. He greeted me warmly and mentioned in passing that
he imagined I must be hungry after a full day of travel. He had
prepared dinner and left a plate in the music school's kitchen for me.

Shocked by his courteous demonstration of kindness in action,
I thanked him, grabbed the plate and headed to my room to unpack
and rest. He smiled and contentedly resumed his work at the school's
desktop computer in the living room where I used to receive his calls.

Over the ensuing weeks and months, we frequently crossed paths at the music school. I continued to rent a room in the back even though I was no longer needed to help oversee things. Sometimes he would leave meals prepared for me when I returned home from work; on other occasions I would practice similar thoughtful gestures. We enjoyed hiking together on the weekends. On Valentine's Day he invited me out for a simple dinner of *baleadas* on a concrete park bench overlooking the ocean.

And, slowly, my heart began to open toward him.

Red Ink, Blue Ink, and Pencil

December 9, 2016

Our fourth Christmas as parents is just around the corner, and the general temperatures have cooled off ever so slightly as the rains visit us more frequently during these tropical "winter" months.

On a recent afternoon, I walked outside under the drizzling rain and came upon a carefully folded-up letter wedged in the door. I immediately knew the letter was from Martian Child. I carefully unwedged the little note and cradled it in my hands for a few moments, wanting to delay the inevitable. I prayed for God to grant me strength to do His will, not mine, and I braced myself for what would come next.

A sense of very selfish dread filled my chest not because I feared some vulgar message or devastating piece of news scribbled inside but rather because I knew Martian Child was right.

I unfolded it and was slightly surprised to see it was not one page but two. Front and back, written in wobbly cursive handwriting that must have taken him all morning to perfect. One paragraph written in red ink, then the next in blue, then the next in pencil. The entire document was written like this. Paragraph after paragraph, the pattern never broke. *Red ink, blue ink, pencil.* At the end of the second page, there were three hearts, one in red ink, one in blue, and the other in pencil.

Martian Child, our beloved teenager who is nowhere near grade-level, who has been hammered by pain and abandonment from a very young age did, in fact, write exactly what I had feared. And worse, for once he was being logical.

I silently considered, *Why can't we just keep on going as we have been since he moved out two years ago — a friendly, mentor-type relationship, but at a safe distance? And our house is so small; we're going to have to start piling people one on top of the other to make everyone fit!*

Even as my ego rebelled against his request, my Father confirmed in my heart what I had known all along: Our prodigal son would be coming home.

However difficult it was to accept, we were beginning to realize that we were the family that God has blessed this young man with, even though we've made our share of mistakes in the process. In spite of ourselves the Lord is growing us to fit the call.

So, through his two-page letter he asked several times and in several different ways — and with several shades of ink — if he could come home. He asked for forgiveness for the times he's disrespected us and not followed the rules. He asked again and again, and it broke my heart even as my mind rattled off its last few objections and then eventually gave up. He wasn't the one who needed to ask for forgiveness; *we were.*

We had been the ones who were too impatient with him, earnestly seeking harvest where we should have been concerned only with sowing.

And so, six days after receiving that multi-colored heartfelt note, Martian Child moved back in with his cardboard box full of belongings. My husband Darwin, Martian Child, and I went to sign all the paperwork that allows him to legally begin living with us again.

Right there in the cramped reception area of that little bubblegum pink government building where we've received all of our treasures, Darwin and I embraced Martian Child bear-hug style with a big grin on our faces that matched that of his. Surely, we displayed the appearance of people who genuinely enjoy one another for reasons that can only be of God.

The middle-aged female lawyer who had received us observed from a careful distance with a curious expression on her face. Why on earth were Darwin and I — and this rogue young man, who had no real stability in his life, so many reasons to be depressed and angry — so joyful, and how on earth did we feel such freedom so as to *hug* him? The majority of the minors who are admitted into foster families or children's homes are *little* children — not towering young men with budding facial hair! Why had this abandoned, broken teenager chosen to find refuge in a Christian family rather than in a gang?

That night over dinner, Queen Bee smiled ear-to-ear and said to the quirky young man whom she has grown to love as a brother, "Welcome home *again*, Martian Child."

Memorable Anecdote

Our teenage son Martian Child in a written reflection
for school:

*Me in the past, I was a cow-herder. I was not a Christian
until I met Darwin and Jennifer. I started to talk with them,
and I became a child of God. I am now a follower of Jesus
Christ. When I was little, I suffered a lot. Now I enjoy
the love of God and I do not ignore people. When someone
insults me, the only thing I do is say, "God bless you." Now
the moments of my life are better than they were before.*

This is My Land; These are My People

My mom's advice and listening ear a constant factor throughout the process of getting to know Darwin, I began sensing that he and I might have a future together. With much prayer, I decided to test my hypothesis.

My plan was simple: on our upcoming hiking adventure I would ask him if he planned on living in Honduras for the rest of his life. If he said yes, I would take that as my sign that we were destined to be friends and nothing more. I was coming up on my one-year anniversary of living on Honduran soil and was planning on moving out to the ranch property within a few months' time, but deep down I had yet to be convinced that I would be spending the rest of my life in this foreign land. Now, if he answered that he would consider moving to another country someday — maybe a safer and more polished place — then, maybe...

We sat down under the shade of a leafy tree, sweaty and adrenaline pumping after having hiked through uneven forested terrain the past hour. We took out our bagged lunch and prayed before devouring the peanut-butter-and-honey sandwiches I had made for the journey. Some Hondurans are reluctant to eat peanut butter, but, oddly enough, it is one of Darwin's favorite foods.

I took a deep breath and tried to venture as casually as possible, "I'd like to ask you a question..."

He spread his arms wide, a big grin on his face and beamed, "Ask me anything!"

His enthusiasm had caught me slightly off guard, but I continued, "Oh, I was just wondering if you're planning on living in Honduras for the rest of your life–"

With chutzpah he answered, nearly cutting me off, "Yes! I love this nation, and these are my people!"

He spoke with emphatic conviction about how God had called him back to serve among his people, but his words had become a blur to me. I nodded politely, trying to mask my disappointment, and thought, *Okay, good for you, Mr. Patriot. I, however, have no idea if I will be living here for the next ten years, much less for the rest of my life. Door closed...*

Team Taga

February 2, 2017

Our precocious Broken Boy, a born sanguine albeit an uncommon one, has been slowly gaining more words in his limited vocabulary since moving into our home two years ago. Upon arrival, the only garbled words available to him were "Pa", "Ma", "Yesh", "No", and "Cow." Literally.

I remember in the early months of his living with us, I would pass by wherever he was playing and ask with eyes wide and sing-song voice, "Broken Boy, *¿cómo estás?*"

Such a simple, loving question, but he was unable to say "well." He would glance up at me, eyes wide with enthusiasm and affection to match mine, stretch his mouth out in an unnaturally wide, wacky grin, and simply nod in affirmation.

I would auto-correct and ask, "Are you doing fine?" It was so easy to forget that all of our inquiries had to be yes-no questions.

To that he would answer excitedly, "Yesh, Ma!" Two of his five vocabulary words.

Over these past many months not only his body but also his verbal skills have begun healing and expanding little by little. He now uses "boom-boom" (car), "beechy" (bike) and "pacho" (excuse me), among others. Due to his unique "accent" and pronunciation of the Spanish words he says, many of our rural neighbors who don't know better think our precious treasure is bilingual and is speaking in English. Others have mistakenly thought he was communicating in Chinese.

Tía Tiki and Broken Boy had formed a special bond in his early months in our family; I often observed her with him and wondered how I, too, could someday connect with (and truly *enjoy*) someone with such limited abilities. Tía Tiki would laugh hysterically with Broken Boy; they seemed to understand and treasure one another beyond reason. Now that Tía Tiki had been away from our ranch for over a year, the Lord was teaching me how to begin loving Broken Boy the way I had seen her love him.

Not too long ago I found myself in our kitchen with Broken Boy, who over time has acquired the loving nickname *Pie*. Even our local students and neighbors know and love him by this title. He has become something akin to a mascot in our school, and our teaching staff and students alike find great joy in being around our quirky boy who occupies a category all his own. Our son never ceases to bring infectious laughter and a sharp wit to any situation, as his social IQ seems to be surprisingly off the charts even if he cannot put his shoes on the right feet and will probably never learn to read and write.

On this occasion he and I were alone in our kitchen. He was sauntering around the counter when he muttered, "Taga" under his breath. Mind you, I'd heard our precious son use this word a few times recently, but I had been unable to pin down its meaning, as there is no common Spanish word that closely resembles it.

I glanced over at him and asked with my eyebrows playfully arched, "Hey, Pie, what's *taga*?"

He bit his lip to contain a huge grin, furrowing his brow intensely as he pretended to think really hard about the mysterious word's meaning. His finger tapping his chin, his lips pursed dramatically, and his head bobbing up and down slightly, he mulled it over in an exaggeratedly intellectual fashion, "Taga..."

I thought I'd help him out, so I started pointing at and picking up different objects in the kitchen. First the soap. I held it in my palm and asked hopefully, "Is this taga?"

He let out a belly laugh, as if that were the most outrageous thing he'd ever heard, "Noo, Ma! Dass *mago!*"

Mago, the Spanish word for *magician*. Of course; soap = magician. I already knew that. Why had I asked?

I pointed at the countertop, the broom, and so on. Each time he answered me in similar fashion. He was unable to identify many of the objects with a specific name, but they were most definitely *not* taga.

I pointed tentatively at myself, asking with eyes wide, "Am *I* taga?"

His toothy grin overtook his little face as he, giggling, shouted, "Noo! You *Ma*, no taga!"

I sighed, "Okay, that's what I thought, but I just wanted to make sure..."

Then I glanced at him furtively out of the corner of my eye and ventured slowly, "Are *you* taga?"

"I *Pie!* I no taga! Ay, Ma..." He shook his head back and forth and brought an open hand up to his forehead, disappointed that I apparently didn't know his name. We both laughed.

I then started acting out verbs, changing parts of speech once taga proved to be something other than a noun. Pie watched my many charades around our kitchen as I acted out walking, singing, and so on, trying to capture the elusive meaning of taga. Each time he would assure me that I was far from finding the definition.

Finally, losing hope, I ventured, "Pie, do *you* even know the meaning of taga?"

He threw up his little arms, laughing hysterically, and howled, "Noo!"

My hands playfully resting on my hips, I shook my head and could do nothing but laugh along with him. What a nonsensical bonding experience!

Later that evening as all the members of our family were present in our kitchen for dinner, I eyed Pie in front of everyone and asked in our new secret language, "Pie, taga?" I had hoped to spark the interest and potential jealousy of the others, as we all try to be the first to learn Pie's new vocabulary words. Although taga meant nothing at all, it was a special secret that only he and I shared.

He caught on to our inside joke immediately and affirmed in an unnecessarily loud voice, "Taga, Ma!"

Several of our kids wondered out loud what taga meant as Tender Heart, Pie's very protective biological sister, stared me down enigmatically. I felt as if I could read her thoughts: *How is it possible that Ma knows my little brother better than me? I'm the one who's closest to Pie; I've been with him since birth. I deserve to be the first one to learn taga! I'll pretend for now that I already know what taga means until later tonight when I'll ask Pie in private for a definition.*

I bit back a smile, shrugged my shoulders, and muttered, "Taga."

Pie kept laughing and bending over, making all kinds of absurd declarations about taga in his shrill, excited tone, and I nodded enthusiastically and added my own crazy taga comments. My husband Darwin and our kids studied our nonsensical exchange and wondered what on earth had gotten into us both. *Taga!*

Let the Balloons Go

Spring 2013

Moments after Darwin had enthusiastically confessed his desire to live and serve among his people for the rest of his life, we concluded our lunch under the tree and began retracing our steps. It would be at least an hour-long journey through vibrant tropical forest before we would reach the highway and take a bus back into the city.

He walked energetically several paces in front of me, commenting to me over his shoulder about a certain toucan on a branch over there and a colorful lizard scurrying over yonder. Honestly, his words were lost on me. I thought I had made my peace about the door being closed on a possible future together, but I sensed the Lord had something to say on the matter.

As I walked in virtual silence, I wrestled internally. *But, Father, Darwin said he never wants to leave Honduras. I can't commit to a marriage if I'm uncertain about how long I'm willing to live abroad; that could have tragic consequences further down the line!*

Sensing the voice I had come to recognize as the Lord's more acutely than I had in months, I felt He replied, *You asked Me for a home, a place to put down roots and serve Me long-term. Is that not what I've given you? The ranch will be your home; you will live and raise the children there. Why are you now so reluctant to accept the life I've designed for you?*

Externally, I continued on the narrow, beaten dirt path several paces behind Darwin. Internally, I was engaged in an epic struggle that just might determine my future.

Then, in my mind's eye I saw a crystal-clear image. It came to me much the same as the vision I had received on the Camino de Santiago in that Spanish hostel almost two years ago. The vision was this:

One of my hands was tightly clasped around the strings that dangled from several helium-inflated balloons. They represented the many other dreams — or rather backup plans — I secretly held for my future if things in Honduras didn't pan out.

The command that accompanied the simple mental image could not have been clearer: *Open your hand.*

My hand, after all, was metaphorically clasped around the strings dangling from the half-dozen or so balloons. Opening my hand was a synonym for letting go. I didn't want to let go of my backup plans. I clasped tighter, scared of losing control. I felt the command came again, as if from the Lord's mouth: *Open your hand and let the balloons go. You can't receive with caring, cupped hands the life I want to give you here in Honduras if you are still clinging to other dreams.*

I continued to follow Darwin's footsteps on the rocky dirt trail, occasionally ducking to avoid leafy branches that hung in our way. I struggled internally for close to an hour before I effectively gave up.

I opened my hand.

In that precise moment Darwin turned around to flash me a large grin before throwing his backpack to one side and spontaneously jumping off a boulder into a river below. I felt the Lord spoke to me and said: *He will be your husband; in him I am sending you a faithful companion and the children a loving father. You don't have to do anything; in My timing everything will fall into place.*

Fast Food,
Fast Family

October 14, 2017

I sat in the noisy McDonald's in Honduras's metropolitan capital city waiting to meet with a new prospective adoption lawyer. Our previous lawyer had done little to inspire us, so we were ready to shuffle cards and pick a new one from the deck. I had just taken a seven-hour bus ride from our ranch home on the other side of the country for my whirlwind tour of the capital to meet with three prospective adoption lawyers.

For over two years now we've actively tried to legally adopt our children, but due to many changing procedures and the child protective agency's lack of time, personnel, and resources, we have gotten nowhere. The agency has even told us that the majority of our kids are unadoptable for legal reasons. Local friends of ours persevered over *six years* just to be able to legally adopt *one* special-needs teenager. To complete all of our adoptions, surely, we'll need an entire lifetime (and a millionaire's bank account)!

My husband and I often feel like we are facing a towering brick wall that extends endlessly in either direction, impotent in our desire to advance. On several occasions I have sadly asked others, never expecting a response: *Why is it so easy to abandon a child (and there is no legal consequence or deterrent for doing so), but when someone feels called to scoop that child up and actually give him or her a permanent family (without seeking personal gain or recognition, but rather doing so out of selfless love), the Honduran government makes it virtually impossible to do so? Shouldn't it be the other way around? Shouldn't the government be thrilled there are stable, loving families who are actually willing to open their homes and devote their lives to raising the nation's abandoned children? Wouldn't opening doors for these families transform a country and provide hope for the future in more ways than one?*

Well, our prospective adoption lawyer had instructed me to wait for him at this noisy food joint. Wealthy, undisciplined teenagers from a local bilingual school gathered in large groups at the tables all around me, too-loud secular music blasted from the built-in speakers above, and a highly choreographed wrestling match blared behind my head on the flat screen television on the wall.

The huge metropolitan city with all of its aggressive sights and sounds is starkly different from our isolated ranch at the base of the mountains. To say the least, I felt awkwardly out of place. Thirty minutes or so passed as I read a book at an empty table in the corner.

My phone rang. I reached for my little device that doesn't have any apps instinctively thinking it was the adoption lawyer calling to tell me he was close by. Thank goodness; I was ready to get our meeting underway and escape the fast-food chaos as soon as possible! My eyes took in the caller identification in one fell swoop as I answered. Honduras's child protective services. Not the capital city adoption lawyer.

I answered to the familiar voice of one of the agency's lawyers. With the amount of abuse, abandonment, and neglect cases in this country paired with the lack of funding and low number of staff on her team, her job is nearly impossible. The government workers are constantly running around frantically, trying to put out forest fires with a squirt gun and slap band-aids on mortal wounds. Although it might be a common tendency to blame the workers for their lack of initiative and efficiency, I've come to believe that many of them are earnestly doing the best they can with the resources they have. It isn't easy.

The lawyer and I exchanged a genuinely kind greeting over the phone, as she and I have worked together on many cases over the years, and she's taken personal interest in our kids' stories.

In that lonely corner of that noisy McDonald's, she popped her question, "Would you be willing to take in two fifteen-year-old girls? *No tienen adonde ir.*"

Through a severely broken cell-phone signal, I could catch about every three words out of five. Need a placement for fifteen days until a permanent solution is found. *¿Sí o no?*

I told the lawyer that I needed to speak with my husband Darwin first. I would call her back the next morning. Naturally, she would have preferred the answer then and there in order to bring the girls over to our home immediately, but she knows that we don't operate like that.

The lawyer agreed to my conditions and we hung up. The adolescent McDonald's patrons continued to hang all over each other; the offensive music continued at high volume; the wrestlers behind me kept up their nonsensical fighting. I prayed silently in the most unlikely of places, asking God what His will was in this situation. He didn't answer immediately, but I did feel at peace. I kept praying.

That evening after finally meeting with the less than punctual adoption lawyer, I called Darwin about the agency's question. I honestly expected him to say no — because of my ill health, because we already had so many other commitments, because of 100 legitimate reasons that any sane person wouldn't want to blindly accept two teenage girls into their home — but he very calmly listened to the scarce details as I presented them to him, and he said yes. And even as the *yes* left his lips, my heart rested in that yes and even jumped for joy.

We hung up the phone. I lay on that antique bedspread of the dear friend's home I was staying in, and I laughed to myself. My eyes traced along the ceiling as I recalled all of my excuses no longer as reasons to say no or to feel scared but rather as the parameters for just one more miracle that God was setting up. He's the God of the impossible, and lately I've been learning that He loves situations where human logic fails, where mortal strength is insufficient and where He can put on a grand display His power.

Two unknown teenage girls? They might arrive on our doorstep pregnant for all we knew. After all, no one in their right mind — in any country! — blindly accepts two suffering adolescents to lock arms with and live alongside for the indefinite future. The government most certainly wouldn't be providing us any family background studies, psychological evaluations, or pertinent behavior information. They may not even have birth certificates or know their real ages. Surely, we have lost our minds and are free-falling into yet one more impossible situation that we trust God will turn into a miracle of grace! My socked feet tapped back and forth in the air as I laid spread out in that quiet upstairs room, considering the impossible.

And, in the depths of my heart, I secretly knew something (or maybe only wished it): The girls wouldn't be staying with us for fifteen days until a permanent solution was found; our family was the permanent solution God had in store for their lives.

Whirlwind Courtship

Spring 2013

Several weeks later, Darwin formally asked me to be his girlfriend.
My heart sunk, as I had hoped and assumed that he would ask
me to marry him after a focused period of courtship. I couldn't
help thinking, *Be his girlfriend? I don't want to be anyone's girlfriend;
I would rather get married or remain single. All the in-betweens just seem
confusing.* I knew of dating relationships that sometimes dragged
on for several years, and I just didn't feel like I had that much
time. I would be moving out to the ranch in a few short months,
and I didn't want to be unnecessarily connected to a potentially
directionless long-distance dating relationship.

I accepted his proposal to be his girlfriend, albeit hesitantly. Darwin
gave me a warm hug and then asked if he could kiss me. I froze.
I had never been kissed before — yes, at age twenty-two, believe it or
not — and had no idea how to react under the given circumstances.
I was just about as virgin as they come. I had hiked mountains in
Argentina, stayed in European hostels, and moved to a third-world
country. My college roommate and I had even smuggled an elderly
homeless woman into our college dorm room on a cold winter
night so that she'd have a warm place to sleep. But a romantic
relationship? That was way out of my league. I muttered some

incoherent excuse, my heart racing faster than Seabiscuit, and left poor Darwin hanging. I was scared to death.

Over the ensuing days I tried to avoid all contact with Darwin, which made for many awkward and uncomfortable encounters. I knew I was ruining everything, so I called my mom for advice. She had been praying for us and rooting us on from afar, a new role for her in my life. She had met Darwin personally while he was in Texas; she had no qualms about him potentially becoming her son-in-law. She encouraged me with what could have become dangerous advice if taken to an extreme, "You are a very brave girl. You've done a lot of brave things and followed God when it wasn't necessarily easy or popular. *Now you've just got to be brave in this new area.*"

I laughed nervously and thanked her for her rather audacious advice. *I've just got to be brave*, I thought. I repeated my new motto over and over throughout the day to gain strength. *Just gotta be brave.* I knew I had to make a move fast so as not to discourage Darwin altogether. I had virtually given him the cold-shoulder ever since he asked me to be his girlfriend. Some dating relationship we had!

That evening, with fear and trembling, I would make my move. I had found a romantic Andrea Bocelli album Teresa had left behind. It was simple enough: after the music teachers and students left the conservatory in the late evening, I would ask Darwin to dance with me. It was not too risky, but it was enough to let him know I was interested and willing to try the whole romance thing.

I sat in the conservatory's living room waiting for him. The problem was, he was taking a really long time. Was he sweeping the back patio or involved in some maintenance project out in the shed? I was too nervous to go look for him, and my resolve was quickly fading. Surely this was all a big mistake; being brave was just too scary.

After what seemed like an eternity, he returned to the music school's living room, keys in hand as he was ready to lock up for the night.

He looked visibly surprised upon seeing me perched on a wooden stool near the front door. Before I lost the nerve, I perked up and said with a shaky voice, "Hi! Do you want to dance with me?" Whew — I did it! I was brave!

He looked stunned beyond belief and somewhat concerned, "W-what?" He stammered.

Oh no! I had to be brave all over again and say my big line a second time! My heart threatening to explode from my throat, I repeated, now less sure, "Do you want to dance with me?"

He accepted, still looking entirely caught off guard, "I didn't think you would still be here. I thought you'd long since gone to your room."

I ignored his comment, got up from my stool, and hit *play* on the little CD player that used to be Teresa's. Darwin is a wonderful dancer, and he reluctantly extended an arm to take me into a close yet respectful slow dance position. (I think he still couldn't believe what was happening.) We stayed like that for a long time, swaying back and forth together as one song gave way to the next. Being brave wasn't so hard after all!

And three months later we were married on a remote nature reserve close to the town Darwin grew up in.

Our friends and family members arrived on a series of small boats through a mangrove swamp. Darwin's family largely outnumbered mine, as he is the youngest of eighteen siblings. My college roommate, who had since become a licensed minister, would be conducting the outdoor ceremony in both Spanish and English. Our new missionary mentors would be sharing a few words. Darwin's music teachers and students would be playing live music at the wedding; his family members would be preparing the big outdoor lunch. After the ceremony, Darwin and I would change clothes and present a choreographed hip-hop routine to Whitney Houston's *I Wanna Dance With Somebody* that we had been practicing for weeks.

I rode up to the wedding site in the long white gown that my mom had made for me (having taken my measurements by phone a couple months prior), both of my parents by my side. Several violinists floated alongside us in kayaks, playing Pachelbel's *Canon*.

As my dad helped me out of the small boat and I began walking the aisle in a moment of pure serenity — feeling as if I was living someone else's life — I thought with a twinkle in my heart, *Mystery Man got his wish.*

A Daredevil
and a Calm Sea

October 16, 2017

Yesterday the large government vehicle roared up to the chain-link front gate of our ranch, and I stood waiting as a ball of hopes and nerves to extend the initial greeting to two young women whom we hoped would become long-term members of our household. My husband Darwin and I would now be parents to ten.

They slipped out of the cab of the truck looking visibly cool, neither scared nor overtly interested in all the implications of such a life-changing move. New town, new home, new family and, soon enough, new school. All without any consistent person in their lives beyond each other. After separate childhoods all over the map, the two treasures had been in the same foster home for a couple years and then were transferred together to a large temporary orphanage a couple weeks ago. I couldn't fathom how I personally would have reacted if I had been placed in their shoes, but I imagined after having bounced around so many times, "new beginnings" perhaps lost their glimmer and proved to be less than they promised to be. I could sense they were jaded and mistrusting, and I couldn't blame them.

Nonetheless, I felt I loved the girls even before meeting them, and beyond logic I was convinced God had chosen us to be their last stop. We would fight to make this *home* for them. No more moves; no more trips in government vehicles with all the girls' belongings stuffed in their backpacks. What they needed were *parents*, not temporary caretakers or a rotating orphanage staff, and my husband and I were determined to earn their trust and find our way into their hearts over time.

I had been told their names were *Daredevil* and *Calm Sea*, but I didn't know which was which. I approached them with a huge, sincere grin on my face and, in one fell swoop, asked if I could give them a welcome hug. The girl whom I would soon learn to be Daredevil, looked at me in utter shock for a moment but then agreed hesitantly to receive my hug. Calm Sea showed no enthusiasm or warmth but accepted my affectionate greeting without complaint.

I exchanged a few polite words with the government personnel before they would soon zip back off down that long gravel road. This was not our first rodeo, and we enjoyed a certain level of mutual trust and appreciation with the agency's staff that had been forged over the years. They didn't need to walk the girls in and make sure they would be fine in their new surroundings; they knew my husband and I would eagerly take care of that. The social worker's kind eyes sparkled as she gripped my hand affectionately, sharing the same belief as I, "*Les va a encantar vivir aquí.* They're home now." I thanked her for her kind words and assured her that we would not be needing to change the girls' placement in fifteen days as the agency had originally told us. Hope shone forth from the social worker's face as she bid goodbye and rolled up her window.

A couple of our treasures and I offered to help Calm Sea and Daredevil with their limited baggage, and they agreed numbly to a tour around our home. Daredevil's bored eyes swept the inner area of our seventeen-acre property where our colorful home, school, and office buildings lie with an expression of *been there, done that*. I could tell by the way she looked at me, eyebrows raised defiantly, that she was sure she already had me and this whole place figured out. She wondered how long she would have to stay before being shuttled off to her next "home."

After enthusiastically giving the girls a tour, I sat down with both of them at a concrete table under one of the trees in our quiet front yard. I longed to connect with them, to *know* them, but I knew it would be a long, delicate process. These hardened, broken hearts would need months and possibly years to soften and heal. I asked a few surface-level questions — not wanting to dig too deep too quick — and talked a bit about myself, my husband, our family, and our sincere desire to form part of the girls' lives long-term. I spoke passionately about God's love and His good plans for the girls' future. Daredevil's eyes wandered around the property beyond me, her interest placed anywhere but in my attempt to communicate in a loving and personal manner with her. Calm Sea half-listened, but her eyes seemed to gloss over. The warm welcome chat had done little to shake them from their stupor, but I refused to be discouraged.

Time, Lord. All we need is time. Please help my husband and me to get through to them with Your love. I trust You brought these two to us for a reason, and in time I long to see them transformed into redeemed daughters.

A few hours later at dinner the girls seemed to loosen up a bit and even revel in the nearly undivided attention the rest of our kids paid them. Daredevil had no trouble conversing freely about all the places she'd been and things she'd seen and done. She was a self-proclaimed seasoned expert on many things. My husband and I glanced at each other, sensing that perhaps certain aspects of her past were being embellished for the purposes of impressing her new housemates, but we decided not to interfere in that moment. We were just glad she was talking, and we would listen and glean what we could in this first stage of getting to know her.

Calm Sea nervously shuffled between our dining table and the kitchen counter nearly a dozen times throughout dinner without any apparent motive, as she was obviously struggling to settle down and be at peace in her new surroundings. Daredevil, unmoved by her companion's restlessness, kept proclaiming all of her feats to any and all who would listen. Several of our kids were enthralled by her words, and if I hadn't known better, I might have thought she had been right there with Cristopher Columbus the day he discovered the Americas.

Then, unexpectedly, she began bragging about her siblings, which caught me off guard completely. *Siblings?* The agency had breathed no mention of siblings for either of our two new girls. (But, then again, the agency had breathed no mention of *any* pertinent personal or family history beyond their first names and ages, of which they got Calm Sea's wrong by one year.)

Feeling as if I had been shoved from behind into quicksand, I probed with my heart picking up speed, "May I ask where your siblings live, Daredevil?"

She was pleased to indulge my questions. As she described the children's home in detail, I recognized it immediately. My husband and I knew the couple who ran the home. It was a Christian ministry and safe, loving environment for the couple dozen children under their care.

She continued on about how great her siblings were and how soon she would be living with them. I silently got swept up in a wave of confusion. *Why had she and her siblings been separated all this time? Why was she here if they were there?* I knew the Honduran government tried to keep sibling groups together at almost all cost. My heart grew sad as I realized that she probably would be here only fifteen days before they would send her off to live where her siblings were placed. Maybe we would not grow to be her permanent family after all.

I couldn't shake the sense that there was something more to the story — something she was leaving unsaid — but nonetheless I tried to assuage her fears, even if she wasn't showing them, "We're so happy for you, Daredevil, and we know you'll really enjoy living with your siblings once the agency moves you there. My husband and I know the directors, and they are wonderful people–"

She cut me off absentmindedly, assuring, "Oh, I know. I used to live there."

The house of cards that I had been meticulously constructing for the last hour in regard to this young woman's story came crashing down in an instant. I glanced over at my husband with silent shock registered on my face. *She used to live there? More importantly, why was she no longer there?*

She continued, apparently with the ever-present goal of entertaining the captive audience she found in the rest of our kids, "I grew up there for several years. It's great; I used to go pick oranges and other fruits from the groves each afternoon. There were so many I didn't know what to do with them all. The property has a river running right through it. I used to jump into it off the big rocks. Everyone else was scared to jump except me." Several of our kids stared at her in a trance, as if she were a queen bordering on the status of goddess.

My husband and I saw through the smoke screen but decided not to interfere just yet. She was definitely hiding something, but we didn't want to embarrass our new arrival in front of our other kids, nor did we trust she would give us an honest answer if we confronted her directly.

In the midst of the impressive dinnertime show, I silently made a mental note to call the source and investigate the truth the very next day.

Memorable Anecdote

Our daughter, Distance-Keeper, wrote the following in a school essay:

One day Martian Child and I were in a verbal spat on the porch, so Pa Darwin came and sent us both out to the yard to pull up weeds for a good while. I have a phrase that I invented: "Sometimes hard things happen, but it's better to shut your mouth."

Thrifty Honeymooners

Summer 2013

After saying our vows in Spanish and English, we escaped to the only natural lake in Honduras for nine days of hiking and exploration. We laughed hysterically while paddling in circles in a cumbersome rowboat, got lost on a remote hiking trail through a mosquito-infested rainforest, and ate the cheapest food we could find. We had spent virtually nothing on our wedding in order to enjoy an extended, albeit barebones, honeymoon. Although by the time we returned from our honeymoon I had acquired a nasty tropical virus and felt on the verge of collapse, our time away had indeed marked a new beginning together as a married couple.

My school year had finished up and with many tears and warm hugs I bid my horde of naughty first-graders goodbye. I would return to that urban bilingual school the following year, but on a part-time schedule to accommodate the new demands I would soon have on my time.

During summer break, Darwin and I would slowly make the transition from living in the city to settling into our new home out on the ranch about half an hour's drive away. Darwin had closely observed Teresa throughout the process of purchasing the ranch property and constructing the little buildings, and he had even been intricately involved on several occasions. In many ways he was much more familiar with the ranch and its history than I was.

We paid off and cut up the only credit card we had between the two of us and started making increasingly thrifty financial decisions together. We would move Teresa's old double bed out to the ranch so that we wouldn't have to buy one, and much of her old, abandoned furniture would likewise be coming with us. Darwin would continue to commute into the city to direct the music school, although over time he would probably transition out of the principal leadership role in order to dedicate himself more fully to the blossoming work at the ranch.

Tía Tiki would be arriving in the fall to accompany us on the journey. Shortly after her arrival, we planned on receiving the first children into our patchwork family.

Facing the Tsunami

October 17, 2017

The very next morning, I drove Calm Sea and Daredevil, our new treasures, into a nearby town where they had been enrolled in public high school. The traditional Honduran school calendar runs from February until November, and the child protective agency had asked us to ensure that both girls finished out their school year where they were enrolled.

My husband and I willingly obliged, working out a tag-team carpooling schedule between the two of us to manage our new girls' last few weeks of public-school education before we would begin educating them at home next year. Even though I was educated in the jungle of the American public-school system, I'd discovered over the years that many Honduran public schools are in a whole other league. We didn't enjoy the idea of our daughters spending several hours per day in the midst of what is generally educational anarchy, but we were given no other choice.

I zipped down the highway with Calm Sea and Daredevil quietly squeezed behind me in our truck's cab. We had met and become instant family less than twenty-four hours prior, and although I was eager to listen to and get to know them, they did not seem to be the least bit interested in connecting with me.

As we pulled up to their public high school and the girls began exiting our truck, the passenger door wide open, one of their friends came up to greet them. Their friend was notably intrigued to see them being unloaded from an unknown vehicle and peered inside to see who was driving. In response to her friend's unsolicited curiosity Daredevil spread her arms wide in an unnecessarily enthusiastic gesture and then pointed at me, saying loudly, "Let me introduce you to my new aunt! Her name is Jennifer!"

I felt awkward and strangely humiliated as my girls' friend stared at me with an overtly confused and displeased expression pasted on her face. I knew Daredevil was nervous and probably felt equally humiliated, as most teens live with their parents or blood relatives and don't change households and "aunts" out of the blue. Surely her friend wondered, *How on earth did Daredevil and Calm Sea get a new "aunt" all of a sudden, and a notably foreign one at that?*

"Aunt", after all, can be a benign term in Honduran orphan culture that simply refers to a woman who takes care of someone without parents. Daredevil and Calm Sea had had many "aunts," a few who had grown to be like loving maternal figures in their lives and many others with whom they enjoyed almost no connection at all. We have never forced our children to call us "Pa" and "Ma" but rather let them choose the title they are most comfortable with. Nonetheless, her outlandish introduction of me as "Aunt Jennifer" had seemed phony. I smiled awkwardly at her perplexed friend, unable to offer any additional explanations.

With that my new daughters grabbed their friend by the arm and were out of sight without so much as turning to say goodbye. I stayed parked until I saw they had entered the school's complex, but even so I felt uneasy. I knew too well that many public schools here cancel classes unannounced and leave students unsupervised for hours at a time. Just that morning our girls had commented to me that several of their female classmates had made a habit of meeting up with older men who jump an isolated part of the school's back fence.

As I turned my car around and began my drive back to our ranch, I took out my cell phone and looked up the director's number of the children's home where Daredevil's siblings lived. *Bingo.* I breathed deep and whispered a quick prayer, finally alone in the car and in a position to seek answers from a reliable source.

Light rain droplets began falling on my windshield as I drove down the highway. I turned my windshield wipers on low and braced myself.

After informing him of the purpose behind my call, the director sighed with obviously strong emotions and began sharing with me the tragic string of events that led to Daredevil's permanent expulsion from their children's home. My stomach sank and I fought back tears. In our household we had been through hell and highwater as we accompanied each of our children in the messy process of healing from their traumatic pasts, but we had *never* faced such a threatening tidal wave as this. I felt that it had already begun crashing over me and I was quickly losing sight of the sun.

If the Lord had called us to set up a rescue shop within a yard of Hell, surely this particular mission would carry us within an *inch* of Hell. I contemplated the intense heat of the nearby flames wearily, wondering how deeply marked our battle scars would be once the burns inevitably healed.

I pulled to a stop not at home but in front of a little grocery store a couple miles before my final destination. The rains had picked up speed and the torrent beat all around me. As our conversation came to a close, my insides pounding violently, I thanked him in the most composed way I possibly could for his help on the matter and we hung up. Then, I slammed my fists into the steering wheel several times in agony as hot tears burned my eyes and cheeks. I let out several guttural screams, alone in the parked car under the pounding rain, and cried out in anguish to God.

I moaned and wailed as the rains drowned out my vision of people walking and biking past my parked car. I unleashed my agony both for Daredevil's tragic past and for the confusing, threatening maze our family had been thrust into by accepting her into our household. The pain, sin, and suffering of this world seemed to be closing in on me in a very real way, and I knew not how to relieve that which hammered within me. Exhausted, I let my forehead fall onto the steering wheel and stayed in that defeated position until I felt capable of completing the rest of the drive home. My spirit felt broken beyond measure, and the high hopes I had enjoyed the day prior seemed to have been drug irreparably through contaminated mud.

Several minutes later as I passed through the chain-link gate onto our ranch property, I could see dozens of the students in our growing school darting about on our large front lawn playing riotous recess games. I contemplated their innocence, freedom, and joy with a heart weakened by the knowledge of tragedy, of innocence stolen. I parked our old pickup in front of our home at the far end of the little row of rainbow-colored cinder block buildings and slid almost lifelessly out of the driver's seat, wanting to disappear into our home without being noticed.

Later that evening, after a very decisive discussion between my husband and me, we asked to speak with Daredevil in private. She rolled her eyes in response to our request but ultimately accepted and followed us into our room.

Daredevil seemed uncomfortable with such an informal setting as she reluctantly took a seat on our bedroom floor across from us. Her eyes traveled around the limited space my husband and I share, possibly trying to see what kind of secret goodies we held out of the kids' reach. After a few brief moments of sweeping the room with her calculating gaze I could tell in her expression that she found nothing of interest.

Softly asking for her to look us in the eyes, I ventured, my voice slightly trembling, "Daredevil, we want you to know that we will never lie to you, and we will do our best to be as upfront and transparent as possible. We want you to know you can trust us."

She seemed unimpressed by this declaration, but my husband nodded slightly, giving me strength to continue, "Yesterday evening over dinner as you were talking about your childhood spent in the ministry where your siblings live, we both found it odd that you are no longer there."

Her eyes suddenly snapped up and she stared at us, visibly nervous about the fact that we might have suspected something. Glad to at least have her attention, I continued as succinctly and lovingly as possible, "So today after I dropped you and Calm Sea off at school, I called the director of your old children's home."

Her face registered both shock and fear. I reached out to place my hand affectionately on her knee as I added the final blow, "And he told me what happened. We know why you're no longer allowed to live there. We know the truth."

What a conversation to have with someone who arrived in your life only a day prior! But could a matter of this weight be put off for later? Surely, we needed to establish a firm foundation with her before too many days had passed.

She stared at us both with unwavering eye contact for several moments. It seemed like none of us moved or breathed as she searched our faces for some glimmer of judgement or moral superiority. She found none, and thick tears welled up in her beautiful dark brown eyes. All of her bravado having been stripped away in an instant, she must have felt naked and utterly vulnerable before us. She did not protest or play the victim card; she did not speak poorly of the director of her old home or call him a liar. She denied nothing; she simply nodded ever so slowly and began to quake slightly, letting her gaze drop to the lifeless tile floor between the three of us.

My husband and I continued, my hand still lovingly placed on her knee, "Daredevil, look at us, sweetie. We are not going to return you to the child protective agency. We know you don't understand it or believe us yet, but we love you and truly believe God brought you into our lives as a beloved daughter. We are your new home and permanent family."

She began to tremble even harder, and large tears began cascading down her silky cheeks. She was making eye contact with us and, more importantly, all three of us were being *real*. I appreciated and felt closer to *this* Daredevil much more than the impressive, yet phony, one I had seen at dinner the night prior.

Darwin and I concluded, "We love you, Daredevil, and we want to see God redeem you and give you the ultimate triumph."

At that point, I scooched over right next to her and asked gently, "Can I give you a hug?" Oh, that seems to be the question I'm always bothering her with!

She nodded yes, and I embraced her in a loving side hug. Her head immediately dropped to my shoulder, and she even extended one of her arms around me and began stroking my back softly, which I had not expected. My husband Darwin remained close as our new Daredevil and I enjoyed that mother-daughter hug for several minutes, her sobbing as much out of shame as out of relief. She did not have to keep secrets from us or expend unnecessary energy trying to deceive us about her past; we knew all the gory details and even so loved her and refused to give up on her.

At the end of our conversation my husband and I prayed for her before I walked with her back to her room. I gave her another hug in her doorway, and we stood in a comfortable embrace for several long moments before I gave her a kiss on the top of her head, and she disappeared onto the other side of her door curtain.

Still shaking slightly after the intense happenings of the day, I thanked God in my heart that He had helped us take the bull by the horns and lay an honest, loving foundation with Daredevil. Surely if we all made it through the next several months intact, we would look back and consider this one of God's powerful miracles.

Memorable Anecdote

Our daughter, Queen Bee, wrote the following in
a reflection essay in school:

My parents have heavily impacted my life. They have been my counselors and teachers. They have shown me their love, something that not all parents do. I have had many struggles, but even so they love me. They correct me; they discipline me; they give me advice. Each day I am walking with them towards God. They have taught me to not fear in this world, to love others without taking notice of their defects, to walk in the light, to not lie, and to protect myself for my future husband.

Blood Beyond the Gate

October 27, 2017

This morning as my husband Darwin came walking through our front door at his usual time after milking the cows, he announced in a disturbing monotone, "The cows are gone."

I stared at him, not understanding what he was trying to say. After all, it is fairly common here for twig fence posts to break and barbed wire to need occasional repair. Our cows had escaped several times for this same reason, and we'd had to go out into our rural town searching for them. I asked dumbly, "What? Which ones?"

"*Las dos vacas lecheras.* Someone stole them."

A sting of panic shot through my veins. *The two adult cows? The two who provide us with milk every morning? Why did he say that someone had stolen them?*

Darwin continued, showing no emotion in his baggy, mis-matched farm clothes, "They killed and butchered them. I found the black cow's head thrown out by our front gate."

Not lost, not stolen, but dead? The only thing I could manage to ask in my numbed state was, "Aren't they worth more alive than dead?"

After all, people kill adult *bulls* for meat; not female milking cows in their prime. Every farmer knows this: female cows are of incredible worth *alive*, for they reproduce, thus giving off a legacy of both offspring and milk. *¿De veras alguien las mató?*

I could only stare at Darwin as my body seemed to shut down. By his appearance he was having a similar reaction. We called together our ten treasures, all standing in a circle in our little living room, holding hands, and did what humanly doesn't make sense — we gave thanks. We cannot, after all, choose to accept only the good from God's hand and not also the bad.

Through tears we thanked God for the milk and calves He had provided us through those cows over the last several years. We likewise unleashed the longing in our hearts for the coming of the God of justice who will turn this upside-down world right-side up.

We then put on our boots and rain jackets and headed outside. We walked in silence out to our front gate and, just beyond, found the severed head of our strong, beautiful, black milking cow. Her eyes were squinted shut in what I considered a grimace of pain. Blood was everywhere.

A few paces away in an open field we found the bloody hides of both cows. Our night watchman's family who lives on our ranch with us came out to the scene as they, too, looked on in solemn disbelief.

Last night we heard no ruckus, no screams from our innocent cows who deserved a peaceful death in old age. The thieves had chopped them up in silent dexterity, taking the meat and leaving behind what was of no use to them.

And now we are left with two orphaned newborn calves — and no milk to feed them.

Over the past four years of living here in rural Honduras, we had given many honest attempts at organic agriculture only to experience similar results with thieves who would break in and steal right before the harvest. The problem of theft is compounded by rocky, oftentimes infertile, soils. Thus, the honest and caring cultivation of cattle seemed to be the answer the Lord had led us to. They graze on our grassy property and enjoy a healthy free-roaming existence, and we could potentially support a small part of our ministry needs through them. Now all of that was put into question.

With these thoughts floating about my mind, about an hour later I walked in boots and rain jacket down that long gravel road from our ranch to the local police station to report the case.

I found one lone police officer standing idly along the highway, so I approached him and numbly explained our tragedy. He listened half-heartedly and informed me sarcastically that that's just how Honduras is. He pointed a finger toward the little bright yellow police station a block away, telling me to leave an official written report (which then gets filed away and typically never dealt with). I walked under a constant drizzle to that little yellow building and knocked on the door several times. No one answered.

I began my long walk back up through our rural neighborhood to our property, which lies on the furthest outskirts of our little town. I advanced in silence, contemplating the beauty of our Lord in the stillness of my own heart. Oh, the promise of the Lord's perfect and final justice is so precious in the face of such gross injustice!

Along the path I found a materially poor family whose property neighbors ours. I carefully informed them of what had happened and encouraged them to keep a close eye on their own small herd, as the five or six cows they have are their main livelihood. I prayed with them, putting the entire situation — our very lives, homes and food sources — into God's hands.

This morning as we stood staring at the bloody hides thrown out in the field, Darwin made the interesting and yet daringly obvious observation, "Yesterday they were alive, and now ... they're dead." Is this not the case for every one of us? Today we are alive — all is well; we expect a great and long future ahead of us; we may even act as if we're going to live forever — and we may very well end up dead tomorrow or at any unexpected moment along the way. Life is so fragile, and in this world nothing is promised. Christ is our life and our salvation.

Dancing Barefoot
to Andrea Bocelli

November 4, 2017

Our four-year anniversary of parenting came and went three days ago without much hoopla. In the beginning, surviving four *days* or four *weeks* deserved thanksgiving and celebration; now we've reached the four-*year* mark almost without a blink. I suppose this is normal.

Two times in the past month my husband Darwin and I have organized a "date" in the living room of our little cinder block home to dance together to romantic music. The first time this happened was several Saturdays ago.

In the early evening I took a shower, shaved my legs (a luxury that I oftentimes don't have time for!), and put on a new, black sleeveless dress. Casual but classy, reaching beyond my knees. I put on a pair of simple silver dangly earrings and headed barefoot out of our bathroom.

As they saw me, each of our treasures had a very similar reaction, "Ma! Wha--? *¡Qué bonita!* Where are you going?"

Normally after a long day, I take a shower and put on my old oversized pajamas that are less than flattering. Never had I gotten all dolled up on a Saturday night without having a specific plan of going somewhere special (which rarely happened anyway).

I laughed at each one's sincere reaction, thanking them for their nice comments and telling them with a twinkle in my eye that I had a date scheduled with my "bofen" that evening (thanks to Chopping Block, that's what I now call Darwin to make our kids laugh). We were going to dance.

They seemed intrigued by this juicy information. I glanced over at our blossoming teenage daughter Tender Heart and said with a twinkle in my eyes, "You know, it was dancing that your Pa and I had our first kiss."

Her eyes widened in shock and she scolded, *"Ma!"* I laughed and shrugged innocently.

Moments later, several of our teen girls (we currently have *seven* daughters ages eleven to seventeen) sat squeezed together like sardines on the little couch in our living room, eyes sparkling expectantly. They could barely contain their excitement as they elbowed one another and leaned toward us with bright faces, *"¡Estamos listas!"* Queen Bee and Daredevil clapped with joy. They thought we were going to put on a show!

Darwin and I both laughed as he got the CD player ready. He had showered and changed, sporting a nice, button-down, teal-colored shirt and black slacks with his hair neatly combed. He looked very handsome. We were both barefoot.

We laughed at our girls' eagerness to see us dance and lovingly shooed them off to their rooms, much to their disappointment. We told everyone that they were free to watch from their open doorways, but we weren't looking to have an actual "audience" within arm's reach in the living room with us.

The music started and some of our girls squealed. Several excited faces shone from one of our kids' three bedrooms. Others pretended not to be interested in the living room spectacle of Pa and Ma slow dancing, but as I looked over Darwin's shoulder, I could see them stealing glances our way and biting back smiles. Martian Child, our teenage son on the cusp of manhood, stood in his doorway openly studying us both, probably taking notes on how his Pa woos his Ma.

Darwin and I held each other close, our feet moving slowly as we swayed back and forth to the music as one song gave way to the next.

At one point Tender Heart went tiptoeing through our living room — not three feet from us — on her way back to her room after using the bathroom as Andrea Bocelli's voice sang in Spanish of some passionate kiss long overdue. Her eyes grew wide and she squealed in shock (as if she had heard something she wasn't supposed to) and darted into her room, hiding promptly behind her curtain. My "bofen" and I both cracked up as we kept dancing.

The Miracle Dinner: Give It All Away to Make Room for the Impossible

November 20, 2017

My husband Darwin and I stood out just beyond our front gate in a circle with our ten foster children. Although in the middle of the rainy season, the night was clear and brisk. A million tiny lights twinkled above. In a hurting country so deeply marked by tragedy, to look another human being in the eye — and one that does not even share your blood! — and to really feel God's love for that person truly is a sign of our Father's active work in the world.

We all held hands in that blessed circle that night, each person in perfect peace as our treasures waited for what Darwin and I were going to tell them.

Earlier that day Darwin had told me that one of our beloved local students that we've been teaching and mentoring for two years was probably going to have to drop out of our little school in order to begin working full-time. His father had lost his job and his family thus had no means of purchasing food. We knew full well the material poverty his family was in when his father *did* have a job. Several family members live together in a one-room wooden shack with a dirt floor and suffer what we can imagine to be immense daily hardship. And now that our student's father — the sole provider of the household — had gotten laid off, how would they survive?

As Darwin shared this devastating news with me earlier that day, I felt the Lord immediately put an instruction upon my heart: *Share your rice and beans with them.*

For us, rice and beans are not an occasional side dish but literally our steak and potatoes that we eat two to three times each day. It is our daily bread. To give away that which we use to feed many hungry mouths each day would surely be foolish, right? If we were to give away our rice and beans, what would *we* eat?

Even as these logical objections showered my mind, my heart was already convinced and ready to obey joyfully. Participate with the living God as His hands and feet to the most vulnerable? Surely there is no greater privilege than this! Count us in.

Then, completely unexpectedly, I sensed the Lord spoke another command to my heart: *Not only your rice and beans, but also all the other food you purchased this morning.*

Oh, I had made my peace with giving away our bulk-sized sacks full of rice and beans, but also those specialty items I had purchased that same day at the local grocery store? Surely if we gave away all of that food as well, we would be committing a grave act of irresponsibility. It would literally leave us with nothing!

I sensed the voice within saying, If you are asked to carry a load one mile, carry it two miles. *Go the extra mile for love of Me. Don't give just your rice and beans; give it all.*

Oh, how many times do we congratulate ourselves on giving away our leftovers, that which we never truly wanted or needed! We donate our old bike or our clothes that no longer fit, which doubtlessly becomes a blessing to someone in need. But to give away all that we have (that which we truly want and even need) for love of God? Oh, this is pure, raw obedience. This is the kind of stuff miracles are made of! Surely God was making room for the impossible.

Under that beautiful starry night sky in that blessed circle with my husband and our ten treasures, we made the announcement. Carefully, in hushed voices, we informed our children that we believed God wanted to supply our student's needs through us. Our kids listened attentively, some with a sparkle in their eyes.

I spoke, "I felt God told me to give them our big sacks of rice and beans." I breathed as I felt like I was taking a running start as I was about to go free-falling over a giant cliff, "… and all the other food in our kitchen."

That was it! I said what I sensed God wanted me to say! Total peace flooded my body, and all those noisy objections were at once silenced.

My husband and I continued, full of confidence in God's perfect will (even when it goes completely against all human logic), "So, now all of you will head into our kitchen, and whatever God leads you to give away, grab it and we're going to load it up in our truck bed. Remember, we don't give away what we don't like; we give to God the best of what we have."

Their eyes trained on ours, smiles grew on their faces as Darwin and I indicated to them that it was their moment to participate, to act as God's warriors of compassion on the front lines of the war. They squealed and raced off through our front gate and into our kitchen.

Our eldest son, Martian Child, had the cumbersome sack of rice on his shoulder as he carried it laboriously out the door. Others grabbed bananas and just about every food that moments before was sitting idly on our pantry's shelf.

At one point, as the frenzy was winding down, Distance-Keeper reached for a bag of Cornflakes to add to the giving bag. Tender Heart intervened, eyes full of sincerity and joy as she stopped her sister, "Better yet, let's give away the bag of granola. I like the granola more." Oh, she got it! To give away that which one likes more; to give God our best, not our leftovers.

Within a time span of five minutes our kitchen was completely emptied — all but one frozen chicken, some toilet paper and possibly that bag of Cornflakes that Tender Heart left behind. It looked like a ravenous swarm of locusts had desolated our pantry. We bounded out to our vehicle — everyone helping carry bags and load the whole prize up into our truck bed.

We instructed our kids to be as quiet as possible, as this act should be done in secret as the Bible teaches. This was not about us; it was about obedience to God's call to love. Surely there is no greater fun, no greater rush of adrenaline, than to live in a constant gamble for God!

We rumbled quietly down that pitch-dark gravel road to a lonely edge of a pineapple field where our beloved student lives. It appeared that no one was home. That encouraged us, as we would then be able to leave everything in their front yard as a total surprise without being recognized as the ones who were used by God in the process.

Everyone shuffled out of the car and began unloading the food as quietly as possible so as not to alert the neighbors. Oh, what a reverse robbery! Arriving in secret to give rather than to steal!

Once everything was unloaded, we re-entered our old pickup truck in a flash and rumbled back up that rocky trail to our ranch.

I will now share with you the truly surprising part of the whole story.

We joyfully went about our business at home that evening without giving a second thought to our empty pantry. I dove into a deep, lovely conversation with Daredevil, our new treasure who moved in with us last month, and our scheduled dinner hour completely escaped me. As she and I wrapped up our conversation with prayer and a long hug, I glanced at the clock and realized I had not fulfilled my "momma" duty very well (but what was there to prepare anyway?). I assured our hungry kiddos that I would see what I could scrap up to make dinner. Dry cornflakes with salt?

At that moment, Martian Child came through our front door and announced unexpectedly, *"La cena está lista."*

Dinner's ready? My head cocked to one side, eyebrows raised high. I asked, "What? Really? Who made dinner?" (And what on earth did they make? Sautéed squares of toilet paper?)

He clarified, "Old Lady Carminda brought dinner over. Everything's served."

Old Lady Carminda — our night-watchman's extremely short, uneducated wife who works part-time in our school's kitchen during the week but who has no commitment whatsoever to make dinner for our family, much less on a weekend. It was Sunday.

She had no idea that we had just given away all of our food, and in her own household their humble income has to stretch to feed many mouths. It was already late, and she should have thought that we had already eaten dinner. She had never prepared dinner for us before, even after years of close relationship with her. What had prompted her? That is for God to know and for us to marvel at in awe and joy.

I walked — taking careful steps as if on holy ground — into our kitchen. There on our wooden dining room table were two big pots — one with a chicken-and-vegetable soup, the other with hot, fresh rice. Old Lady Carminda had also made fresh tortillas for us. A full meal. And she wasn't even there, beaming with a big smile to see our reaction to her serendipitous generosity.

She — herself a materially poor woman who only has a second-grade education — had simply prepared us an extravagant meal, dropped it off without calling attention to herself, and went on her merry way. It seemed that she, too, understood Christ's command to do good deeds in secret. I stared at the food in silence.

Our kids enthusiastically opened up the pots to take a sneak-peek at what was inside as everyone's stomachs were growling. Our kids squeezed together like sardines around our rectangular table. My heart exploded in a thousand fireworks of faith. Surely this is a miracle of God's provision!

Truly God had led us to give it all away, and truly He had prompted our precious neighbor to prepare food for us even as she had no idea of our act of total obedience. The food was never ours (or hers) anyway; everything is God's, and I believe He loves orchestrating these moments of divine provision if only we are willing to trust and obey.

Preaching Peace Amidst the Protesters

December 2, 2017

Dozens of armed Honduran military agents lined the bridge, stone-faced like statues. Rioters and political protesters gathered close by, screaming violently and waving flags. A large crowd had even formed a circle as one man beat a drum while screaming out his hatred for a certain politician and his love for another.

We tread the burnt ground carefully, our shoes acquiring the sticky black tar from tires that had burned to ash. We asked God silently where our entry point would be. After all, at this same bridge there had been a dangerous riot the day prior, and we had been told a young boy had been shot and killed in the crossfire.

. . .

Our family had awoken this morning at 2:30 a.m. with great enthusiasm, for we were planning on traveling to a beautiful campground several hours away for a youth retreat that promised to be well-suited to the spiritual growth of our foster teens. With hopeful spirits we were determined to attend the conference, fully knowing that many of the bridges we would need to pass might possibly be blocked due to the volatile political situation. Our plan: get up super early and try to beat the protesters to the bridges.

All was going as planned under the cloak of darkness. We zipped quietly down the highway as it seemed that the rioters were still sleeping. We passed nine blockade points without problems.

Our car was packed to the brim with backpacks, props for our skit, snacks for the journey, and worship music playing on the inside of our old pickup's cabin. It looked like our plan just might work: we just might be able to slip by all the drama unnoticed, arriving at our destination before the day's promised chaos commenced anew.

Around 5:00 a.m. we came upon a standstill on the highway. There were dozens of vehicles completely stopped. With optimism still brimming in our hearts, I left our car with its emergency blinkers on and bounded out of the vehicle, jogging up ahead to try to see what we needed to do to pass our tenth obstacle.

As I reached a couple blocks ahead, there was an eighteen-wheeler parked completely perpendicular across the bridge, forming a formidable blockade that could not be passed by any vehicle. I approached the large group of men stationed at the roadblock with confidence and sincerity, greeting them and informing them that I had come in peace and simply desired to pass in order to attend a Christian conference a few hours away.

The men — several of whom had their faces covered with rags or wore Satanic-looking masks — began asking for money and other gifts and started to form a semi-circle around me, affirming that they wouldn't be letting anyone pass anytime soon. I suddenly realized that this roadblock would not be like those which we had crossed thus far.

Sensing danger, I politely thanked them for listening to my request and promptly began running away back toward our vehicle a couple blocks away.

Other travelers informed us that they had already been waiting at that same bridge for two to three days without any budge, and

they were forced to get hotels and go buy clothes and food for
the prolonged wait. Once two gunshots went off close to where our
vehicle sat parked, we took that as our cue and began zipping back
down the road we had just braved in order to return from where
we came from.

We hoped the previous nine roadblocks weren't already taken anew,
lest we get stranded somewhere in between and thus find ourselves
unable to return home.

The rioters had taken up one of the last posts on our journey (all
with their faces covered) and had lit many tires on fire, completely
blocking the passageway. With some polite convincing, they let us
pass, but it was in no way a peaceful roadblock. As the sun was
gaining strength in the sky above, so the anger of the rioters was
gaining force as the day was only just beginning.

Once home safely, we decided to pray as a family about the political
situation and for all involved. We then began singing hymns and
songs of praise, worshipping He who already is our president
and King, He who need not be elected by men and who will be
overthrown by no mortal. We declared our love for God around
that rustic wooden table even as many all around the country were
continuing onward in their fires, protests, and hatred.

During a song, eyes closed, I felt the Lord spoke to me and told me
that our day's assignment wasn't through yet. Even after getting up
at 2:30 a.m. and having spent the last five hours dodging obstacles
and trying to complete our road trip in vain, there was still work
God had for us (beyond prayer). I felt He placed a very clear
command upon my heart: *Go to the rioters. Share My Word and My
love with them.*

Today was, after all, a day when the message of peace and salvation
was most needed. We emptied our car of all our supplies and headed
out with virtually nothing other than our Bibles. We would see where

the Lord would lead us, as surely we wouldn't have to go far to find people desperately in need of a message of peace.

On a day when most sane, peace-seeking people stayed out of the public eye, holed up in their homes in order to avoid any stray bullets or unneeded confrontations with unhappy political patrons, God sent us out.

We decided to return to the last blockade we had passed on our way home, where there had been over a dozen masked, angry men lighting fires across the highway. We headed out in silence, driving about ten minutes west before seeing them on the horizon and slowing down, our hearts contemplative and yearning for God to give us the right words to say (and, for the rioting men, ears to hear).

We parked our car about fifty yards away, slowly got out of our vehicle, hands raised in signs of peace, and began walking carefully toward the flames and masked men. The police had already arrived and were standing idly nearby, serving virtually zero purpose as they neither intervened to remove the highway disturbance nor supported the protesters. Traffic piled up on both sides of the scene, dozens of vehicles unable to pass.

We shouted friendly greetings from a distance to the rioting men, who by now were all watching us and on-guard for any foul play they thought we might pull. We told them that we came in peace, belonged to no political party, and simply wanted to share with them God's Word. I asked if they would let us get closer to them.

Their defensive posture immediately changed as the leader agreed and invited us to draw nearer to the blockade. We approached as the masked men, several women and children suddenly formed a great circle around us, curious as to what we would say to them.

We introduced ourselves by name, likewise asking the names of each present. Some of the men even began taking their masks off, while a couple others lost interest and continued adding more tires to the fire and shouting every time a new car would approach and come to an idle stop. We were standing close to the blockade — the flames warmed our faces — off to the side of the highway with those who were interested in learning the truth, while the ruckus of the world's lies for power and control continued onward not ten feet away.

We read aloud great portions of the book of Romans and shared openly with them of our faith in Christ, that He — and no human president — is humanity's true hope. Queen Bee, Tender Heart, and Martian Child even shared wisdom and godly perspective with them. Two of our teachers, who over the course of the years have become like sisters and friends to me, also encouraged them in the way of Christ.

Some rioters came and went, but two men — one of whom was middle-aged and had been the stand-offish leader of the group at the beginning — stayed with us the entire time, eyes wide and hearts seemingly open. No one was forcing them to listen. At the end we asked if we could pray for them, and they agreed. We even put our hands on them, assuring them that we carried no weapon other than that which is the most powerful of all — God's love. At the end of our time together we shook hands and bid our farewells as we reminded them once more that God loves them and that there is a more excellent way than that of political aspirations and highway violence.

As we turned and left, we felt full of God's joy albeit with a heavy heart. They did not take down the blockade, and only God would have the privilege of knowing what, if any, effect would come about from our obedience. We got back in the car and continued to drive in silence, wondering where God would lead us next. It was definitely the first adventure of its kind for us, and at the most delicate of times.

Driving about ten minutes back east where we had come from, we found the newly constructed blockade in our own town. This group was about four times as big as the first one, and we ended up spending a good portion of time there. We stood on an old metal chair in the midst of the chaos and read Jesus' teachings on loving our enemies as God loved us even when we were His enemies.

So many look to a president or other type of leader to make a great change or heal the nation, but the change begins with each and every one of us as we drop to our knees before God in repentance. That is what will change a nation; hatred and scandal will not bring about that change that so many citizens long for.

Our third and last stop would be that of the main bridge passageway into the city, about thirty minutes east of our town. That last bridge on our agenda was where the young boy had been killed the day prior and where the majority of the political violence was focused. We breathed deep, wondering if it was foolish to head straight-on into such chaos but at the same time fully assured that those were the people who most desperately needed the message of peace.

We arrived and parked several blocks away, walking carefully along the main road over fallen wires, black ash, and sticky tar. Some of our kids had acquired the sticky tar-like substance on their faces, and our noses burned with the unpleasant smell. Multitudes of people occupied the entire block leading up to the bridge, significantly more so than in either of our previous two stops combined.

We hesitated as we approached the bridge, consulting among ourselves as to where we should start. There was no way we would be able to talk with everyone at once, as there were factions of armed soldiers, police, and dozens of zealous rioters. It looked like a war zone that at any point might break out in total chaos (as, in fact, had occurred the day prior). Everyone was on edge, and there were many onlookers.

I asked God in my heart to show me who to talk to.

During this time, the screaming and chanting protesters swept us up into their group and shuttled us forcefully across the highway, probably believing we had come to support them. They waved flags and spat insults at the other group as we smiled politely and kept our mouths shut. We sensed that we would not be able to get a word in with their group, as they were clearly intent on being heard, not on hearing others.

In that moment, I felt God showed me a lone soldier at the end of the bridge who was unoccupied.

I asked the soldier if we could speak with him. Defensive and visibly scared, he asked nervously what we wanted to talk about. We informed him that we wanted to share God's Word with him and give a message of peace in turbulent times. His guard immediately dropped, and he agreed.

At the time I believed it might have been only with this one soldier that we would have an open door, as everyone else was so dispersed and carefully supervising their respective group amidst the overall din. I thanked God in my heart of hearts that this young soldier was available, fully convinced that every life counts and that to even touch one person's life is worth it. Maybe we had come to this busy bridge to share the gospel with this one young soldier.

The soldier left us promptly to consult with his superiors lining the bridge, all fully armed and on guard. He returned to inform us, "You can share the message with the whole group."

They were going to abandon their post! My mouth dropped slightly open, as we had never arrived prepared with a message but rather continuously asked God to put the right words in our mouths. *Talk with the whole armed division on duty? Oh, God, give us the right words!*

Within moments, dozens of the fully armed, uniformed men left the bridge and walked down a small slope where they would be able to hear us more clearly. We had no microphone, no stage and no program.

Others — some soldiers, some protesters and others uninvolved onlookers — began gathering around and behind us as we began to read aloud from the book of First John. *God is love, and He showed us this love by sending Christ to die for us. If we say that we love God, we must also love people (even our enemies).*

People kept drawing near as we read aloud nearly the whole book of First John, encouraging the people to receive God's love and forgiveness through Christ and to begin showing it to one another. People leaned in to hear. Alas, the opposing groups had come together, but not in disrespectful confrontation, but rather as equal recipients of the truth of God, ears and hearts open.

Our teenage son, Martian Child, prayed over the soldiers and common folk with a simple, honest prayer asking for God's will to be done and for the people to put their hope in God rather than in a human president who will never be able to live up to our expectations. He prayed for peace in a language everyone could understand.

As we left, one local man who had heard us preach peace approached and asked that we continue. He affirmed that the Gospel is for the people's salvation and they must hear it.

At that point another man, a rioter on the brink of taking control of the bridge with his angry crew, began shouting, "Get God's Word out of here! ¡No queremos la Palabra de Dios aquí!"

It sent chills down my spine, not because I feared that man but because that is, in fact, the attitude at large in the world today. We shake an angry fist at the eternally good God and scream in our own misery, "Get God's Word out of here! We don't want Him in our lives! Ban Him from our government; remove Him from our schools!" If only we truly believed that He came to give life in abundance and joyfully submitted our lives to His perfect will, we might finally experience that joy and peace that we so long for (and seek in all the wrong places).

Well, at the end of our expedition, twelve hours had passed since our 2:30 a.m. get-up. We felt spent, like soldiers after coming back from war. Joyful. Hopeful. Grateful. Fearless.

Rather than learning and growing within the safe, organized context of the youth retreat we weren't able to reach, this was the learning experience that apparently God had in mind all along. To be His peacemakers on the front lines.

Territory Gained; Hearts Conquered

January 15, 2018

The unstable political situation has finally been reduced to
a contained, albeit uncomfortable, simmer after weeks of incredible
havoc, hate crimes, and barricaded highways.

Finally alone after a long planning meeting with our teaching staff
on our ranch property, I contemplated in my heart the recent move
of Chopping Block and Distance-Keeper from our home to the long-
term care of a loving, safe biological aunt. The girls had been with
us two-and-a-half years, and we had believed they might stay with
us forever. When we found their aunt months prior, however, we
could see the warm flame of kindness in her eyes and knew that
with time the girls would transition from our care to hers. She was,
after all, already raising one of the girls' little brothers and was
eager to include her two nieces into her loving, stable family.

Stacking papers in our office and preparing to close things down
for the day, my thoughts shifted as I considered the ways in which
we've evolved as a family over the past few months. Ever since Calm
Sea and Daredevil moved in, my husband Darwin and I have been
making a highly concentrated effort to win our Daredevil's trust and
affections. Due to her tumultuous past, we knew instinctively that

she was going to do something; and that something could either
be something good and for God's glory or it could be something
disastrous. In short, we preferred to have her on our team than to
have her feel alone and misunderstood, which would probably lead to
her rebelling against our authority in the home.

Well, our plan was working incredibly well. Week after week we
were winning more of Daredevil's heart; she was opening up to us,
laughing wholeheartedly at our corny jokes that we would include
her in, and always willing to give and receive sincere hugs. I made
a consistent effort to establish our initial bond, something that our
other treasures took note of and many became jealous about. It
was becoming increasingly obvious that Darwin and I were winning
the title of Daredevil's Favorite People. We were thankful for the
connection we were intentionally establishing with her, but we both
knew that it was not out of favoritism but rather a strategic, loving
move on our part.

Daredevil, however, began taking me not as a maternal figure but
rather as her best friend and equal, an unintended effect of all the
quality time I was spending with her. She would call me by my first
name (I was no longer even 'aunt' to her), and she would use the
informal pronoun *tú* in Spanish to address me rather than the more
respectful *usted*. She even gave me a nickname I was less than fond
of: Jenny. I had won her heart but not yet her respect.

So, on several occasions "Jenny" had to sit down with Daredevil and
lovingly but firmly ask that she use the more respectful pronoun
usted when addressing the adults in her life, as all of our kids
are expected to do. Our conversations produced minimal effect, and
I began to feel frustrated and disrespected by the too-familiar way in
which she was treating me.

Then, a few weeks ago we were visiting the beach as a family for
a few days of fishing, snorkeling, and kayaking. I found myself
sitting cross-legged on the sand across from Daredevil. We were

breaching the topic of *tú-usted* for the umpteenth time, and I took
the opportunity to communicate to her my sincere desire to be
her mom. All of our treasures know they are free to accept us as
substitute parents or simply take us as loving mentor figures, but
our hearts' desire is to act as parents and be accepted as such.
She needed a mother (as each person around the world does), and
I longed to fill that role for her, however imperfectly. I affirmed and
encouraged her as we sat on that shady spot on the sand, asking
her to let me into her life not as a friend but as a mother. She
seemed to half-listen, and I came away from the conversation feeling
like once more little ground was gained.

Later that evening, as I was folding a large, light-blue bed sheet
in the little cabin we were all sharing as a family, a quiet,
unrecognizable voice from behind me uttered the word, "Ma."
Someone was standing in the doorway and seeking my attention.
I froze. I knew the tone and inflections of each of our kids' voices
and the way they each call me "Ma". This one I did not recognize.
I spun around slowly.

Daredevil stood a couple yards away, staring at me in silence with
a serene, vulnerable expression on her face. She was leagues out of
her comfort zone; she was trying out the name to see how it fit.
The empty room around us felt heavy with significance.

I put the big blue bedsheet down and approached her slowly.
I didn't want to make a big deal out of the moment in fear of
scaring her off. I touched her arm gently and asked, "Yes?"

She smiled softly and told me that one of our other kids needed my
help with something. I assured her that I would be right there. Then
she disappeared.

It happened again the next day, and then the name change became
permanent henceforth: Jenny had become Ma, and with it, Daredevil
began simultaneously addressing me with the respectful pronoun *usted*.

A mere day or two later, my heart still full with Daredevil's acceptance of me as her surrogate mother, Calm Sea — who does not normally show up on our radar screen in a blaring way — asked to speak to me in private. We sat together on her bottom bunk in our little vacation cabin near the sea, and she tentatively began pouring her heart out to me. She had not yet accepted me as "Ma," but she did consistently address me in a respectful, appropriate manner.

She had slipped me a hand-written note the evening prior saying that she oftentimes felt left out and overlooked; she felt like I preferred Daredevil over her. My heart sunk as I realized I had thrown about eighty-five percent of my energies into gaining Daredevil's trust and affection while I had dedicated the much more stable Calm Sea a mere fifteen percent. I had assumed the phlegmatic Calm Sea was fine and happy; that was, after all, how she appeared to those around her. She was perhaps the easiest of all of our children and never demanded attention. It was too easy for me to become consumed with the needs of Daredevil, Fireball or even Queen Bee.

And, I realized in the blink of an eye that all of that needed to change. Calm Sea needed to become one of my main priorities just as Daredevil and our other kids were.

So, Calm Sea and I sat conversing on her bottom bunk for a couple hours as the peaceful lapping of ocean waves sounded just beyond. Several of our other treasures came and went from the tiny cabin as they grabbed towels, swim goggles, and books to read on the dock. I would smile at them, answering whatever questions they might have for me before continuing on in my new quest to know and love Calm Sea.

At first our time together seemed forced and uncomfortable, as we knew virtually nothing about one another beyond the basics. I asked many questions; she opened up and began sharing. No fireworks went off in the heavens nor did Calm Sea leap for joy, but we both knew it was a start and there would be many more moments of meaningful connection to come. That much I promised her.

A couple weeks after our initial bonding time, back at home on our ranch and in the thick of daily responsibilities, a little piece of folded notebook paper was slipped under our bedroom door late at night. I got up and retrieved the letter, flashlight in hand.

Unfolding it, Darwin and I noticed it was Calm Sea's handwriting and imperfect grammar. She wrote of her immense love for us and of the fact that she thanked God for having brought her to our family. In it, she confessed her desire to call us "Pa" and "Ma" as she now sees us as her parents but that she still feels too shy and insecure to use the new titles out loud in daily life.

My husband and I smiled and thanked God in our hearts that He had allowed us to win not only Daredevil's affections but now Calm Sea's as well.

A Letter for the Wrong Person

August 28, 2018

Nearly five years into our journey, the possibility of becoming adoptive parents grows bleaker each day due to the many legal complications and delays involving our children's cases, but even so we rejoice in the parenting relationship we have with those the Lord has given us.

A few Saturdays ago, I sat at the wooden table in our family room with Fireball and Daredevil, the front door wide open to let in light and what little breeze there was. Every evening we eat dinner around this same table with its floral-print tablecloth, each person elbow-to-elbow with those next to them. We drag over the piano bench so that there will be enough seats for everyone.

On this particular occasion, the three of us gathered at this table with the intention of working on our 'homework' — my girls on math and grammar assignments; me on planning and administration. I serve as our kids' teacher in an array of subjects, but when we're not in classes I'm just Ma. My husband and I do much role-hopping throughout the week, and with God's grace it has become normal to us.

Through the open front door, I glanced out beyond our chain-link fence to watch our small herd of milking cows roam about our large, grassy property. After the cattle thieves had broken in and slaughtered our two adult milking cows last November, we'd recuperated slowly. Our new momma cow just gave birth recently to a little male calf.

My eyes traced our expansive lawn as I took in the view of the flowering plants and the bright-colored clothes hanging on the clothesline. When the masses leave, this ranch turns into a quiet haven, a peaceful paradise. It is home and ministry to us at the same time. It is the center of our community outreach and school and at the same time serves as my own refuge after long, tiring days of service. I truly love this place and feel at home here.

On Saturdays I move about slower than usual, oftentimes in baggy, old clothes with my wild brown hair up in a messy bun. I reflect, seek God's ongoing direction, remember. I quietly got up from the table and slipped outside.

I stood barefoot on our front lawn, no one looking for me or needing me, as I studied with joy our special-needs son, Pie, as he teetered about our silent, empty yard on his dearly loved but extremely beaten-up bicycle. He can spend hours on that little bike without saying a word, and on this particular occasion he didn't realize I was watching him.

I silently considered the fact that our teenage son, Martian Child, abruptly left our home four months ago, leaving in his wake much confusion in our household. We had already lost him once when he moved out in 2014; our hearts were not prepared to lose him again.

After meandering around the yard a few more minutes, praying silently for Martian Child, I crossed the threshold into our living room, returning to where our two girls awaited me. I took one glance at my to-do pile and realized that I didn't want to do any of it. By the look on my girls' faces, they were thinking the same about their homework.

I grabbed the oil pastels, paper, and envelopes, feeling invigorated. I sat down next to our two girls with a smile and quickly began diving into my unannounced art project. Fireball and Daredevil stared at me silently, mischievously happy to see me acting somewhat like a small child.

The day prior we had held a staff meeting with our small team of teachers, all of whom have become like a precious extended family to us. We had agreed to split up the task of writing individual letters of encouragement, friendship, and spiritual orientation for the few dozen students in our little school. Each child and teen would receive two letters from different people, meaning we would need a total of almost one hundred personalized, creative letters with decorated envelopes.

We feel that God has given us the task of setting a powerful, loving example of just what it means to write a letter under God's perfect will and with His purposes in mind. Our letters come from the mature adults in our students' lives, not from their peers who oftentimes seek affirmation and identity in all the wrong places. One local teen boy commented innocently to his teacher after having received his first two uplifting letters earlier this year, "I had no idea that people could write such kind letters without them being flirtatious or directed toward a dating relationship."

This, after all, has been a big struggle among our students. If and when they do write any kind of personal letter to a classmate, many times it is an inappropriate effort at expressing "love" and "admiration" (bordering on fantasy and obsession) to their crush. We have fought hard against this current, trying to establish a new, biblical norm among our students for male-female interactions. It seems we may be gaining some ground, albeit slowly.

I began decorating envelopes with the oil pastels and expressing my sincere thoughts on paper for these local youth whom I have grown to know and love dearly.

It didn't take long until my girls, too, put their homework aside and asked to borrow some oil pastels. All three of us began creating with great interest, and suddenly several hours had gone by.

Waist-deep in the whole process, I began writing my letter to a very petite and soft-spoken little girl in our small fourth-grade class. She is the younger sister of Team Player, the treasure who lived with us on and off for a couple years and with whom we currently have a tragic history.

After Team Player's mother valiantly (and counter-culturally) left behind her abusive husband in order to regain custody of her daughter, my husband Darwin and I stayed in the picture as Team Player's teachers and mentors and began employing her mom and giving her basic literacy classes. Team Player had been baptized under our care, but the decisions she began making months later did not reflect God's best for her life. She discontinued her education partway into ninth grade and recently moved across the country to live with her lover whom she barely knows.

When I picked up my black pen to write what should have been a very happy, upbeat letter to Team Player's precious little sister, a very unexpected heaviness overcame me, and I had to fight back tears. I didn't see this emotional storm within me coming, as I have remained publicly very calm and rational about Team Player's decision-making and demise over the past couple months. I've kept outwardly cool about something that has actually ripped me apart.

I considered the fact that it is much less painful to stay cool and collected (cynical even) than to allow yourself to feel the weight of the sadness of broken dreams and lost loved ones.

The letter turned out to be much longer than I had originally intended, joyful and profoundly sincere. As a final touch, I drew bright-colored hearts all around the margins. I re-read it several times, thinking each time more about Team Player than about her little sister. *La amábamos tanto, y ahora ya no está...*

A couple weeks later Team Player's mom came up to me with a huge smile on her face, thanking me for the beautiful letter I had written to her pint-sized daughter.

As I remembered fondly the advice and words of living hope that I had written in that sweet little girl's letter, I prayed in my heart that she might believe those words and follow Him, even if her older sister hasn't yet.

Not a Thousand, But One

April 29, 2019

We are in the midst of another scorching dry season. Routine continues to replace adventure; experience has made us more efficient yet, I fear, less sensitive. A few weeks ago, we reintegrated Pie, our special-needs foster son, back into a healthy family situation with his biological grandmother. His older sister, Tender Heart, has decided to stay as a permanent member of our household. Although we miss Pie dearly and oftentimes find ourselves reminiscing about fond anecdotes of our four years spent with him, we remain in close contact and see him regularly.

After having had up to ten treasures in our home at once, suddenly having only six seemed surprisingly easy. The parenting journey thus far has been blessed yet exhausting to the bone, and my husband and I have soft new battle cries for this season: No-more-new-kids and We-want-a-manageable-household.

Then the child protective agency called twice.

I said no both times without giving it a second thought, as receiving new children into our family was not within our short-term plans.

But often our own plans are just that: our plans, not God's. I said my second "no" over the phone to the government social worker, ready to politely hang up. Then, unexpectedly, I felt the Lord led me to consider the possibility of laying our plans — our control — on the altar in the name of love.

Roller Coaster, a thirteen-year-old girl, has already lived as an adult man's live-in sexual partner. Dad's not in the picture. Mom is highly unstable. Needs a long-term, loving family.

As I listened to all the details I probably could have imagined on my own, the social worker began pleading, "We have nowhere else to put her. If you receive her, you would be giving her ... an opportunity at life."

We would agree to meet Roller Coaster, but would make no over-the-phone commitment to take her in. The social worker was ecstatic.

After hanging up, I went directly to our bright purple office building we share with our small local teaching staff. My husband was busy teaching classes, but I found one of our female teachers fairly unoccupied and asked her for prayer and counsel in the meantime. She readily accepted, and we sat down next to each other on the little purple couch in our office's prayer room.

I shared openly and extensively with her, both secretly excited about the possibility of extending "an opportunity at life" to one more person while also tense and scared about all that could go wrong. I voiced my thoughts as she listened attentively. "I mean, we could take her in, but there are thousands of other teen girls in her same situation — dysfunctional family, history of sexual abuse..."

Our beloved teacher nodded, fully aware that in our area of Honduras there are numerous cases of surprisingly young girls who already live with their older "boyfriends" or who daily endure home-lives stained by sexual trauma at the hands of perverted family members. The need is overwhelming, and most cases receive virtually zero attention from local authorities.

I continued, "And, it just wouldn't be realistic to take in thousands of them. *No podemos ser familia para miles de muchachas.*" Our teacher listened as I verbally processed the storm within me.

But in that very moment I felt the Lord struck me deep, making a 180 degree turn in my argument. I said slowly, "But He's not asking us to take in thousands of girls. The social worker called us about one. *Sólo una.*"

I felt like I had surrendered to God's will in one fatal blow. It was a divine TKO. You won, I thought with great heaviness mixed with the first fruits of joy welling up in my heart. I sensed He was indeed calling us to start over again with a new lost daughter of His. Not with thousands, but with just one. And I would obey not only willingly but with a joy that very few can understand.

At the end of our conversation my teacher-friend prayed with me for young Roller Coaster and that the Lord might grant my husband and me the love, strength, and wisdom to accept this new challenge if He should so desire us to take it on. Later that evening, Darwin and I discussed the matter at length and together we decided to proceed because he, too, was in agreement. We both felt peace.

We would soon be parents to six teenage daughters and one preteen son.

That night — about two-and-a-half weeks ago — my husband and I prepared a foam mattress on our bedroom floor for our new arrival. Instead of moving her in with our teen girls all at once, we decided to have her with us for the first week in order to help ease her transition while also forging some semblance of parent-child bond with our new treasure in a condensed amount of time.

We sat down on the cool tile floor next to her mattress and asked if we could pray for her. She said yes. After doing so we tucked her into bed — our teenage-sized new baby! — and gave her a hug and a kiss before climbing into our own bed not three feet from hers. I couldn't help feeling like we were reliving déjà vu after having received little Chopping Block in similar fashion four years ago.

My husband promptly drifted off into sweet slumber as I lay staring at the ceiling in the dark, hot room. My heart raced for joy as I listened closely trying to identify if our new treasure had already fallen asleep or was still as wide awake as I was. *Did she feel welcome and wanted here? Would we be able to form a close bond with time, or would she prove distant and guarded? Would she sleep throughout the night or wake up screaming with nightmares? What if she stopped breathing right there on her mattress?*

My mind raced as I thanked God in my heart for who He is and for leading us on this wild adventure that was never our plan to begin with. The minutes turned into hours, and at some point in the wee hours of the morning I drifted off to sleep in spite of the heavenly joy that I felt might burst right out through my bones.

Following Jesus, Who Sought Out Prostitutes and Sinners

June 20, 2019

In our rural town it is not uncommon for sporadic murders to take place. Oftentimes our neighbors will inform us that a dead body was found thrown out in the local pineapple fields or seen alongside the highway.

Several weeks ago, my husband, our seven foster children, and I were driving slowly in our old Toyota pickup truck through our sleepy town toward the highway. Easter Sunday was approaching.

We suddenly noticed a large crowd of people standing alongside the road. My husband casually extended an arm outside the car's window to point at the crowd, commenting, "Oh, I bet a local church is doing some kind of Easter parade for the resurrection."

He slowed our car's speed to a crawl as all of us began studying the crowd. I began waving at the people, extending a friendly greeting as I searched for familiar faces among them. After all, we know many people who live in this area of our town, and it wouldn't be surprising if a few of our students were in the crowd.

Rather than return my greetings, everyone just stared blankly. In the midst of their gloom they hardly looked like they were triumphantly celebrating Christ's resurrection.

Darwin was the first to notice the dead body covered haphazardly with a bloody bed sheet right there in someone's front yard. He muttered something under his breath and sped up the car in order to move us past what he realized was not a parade but rather an unresolved crime scene.

I glanced over at him, searching his face for clues, and then whipped my gaze back out the passenger's window when I realized what he had seen. I let out a slight gasp, looked away, and immediately stopped what I realized had been highly inappropriate waving as chills covered my body. Our daughters who were inside the cabin with us grew silent as we all registered the tragedy.

The police station is located only a few blocks away, but there were no police to be found among the somber crowd.

We continued onward in silence for several minutes as we all wondered who had been killed and why. Was it gang-related? Or did two late-night drunks simply get into a scuffle that escalated into much more than they had ever intended? Was it a meticulously planned murder, or was it a crime of passion that developed in the blink of an eye?

Not two weeks earlier another dead body was seen (this one uncovered) along the same road. My husband had been shuttling a group of our preteen students up to our ranch for another day of classes and discipleship when he came upon the corpse. Darwin was saddened to witness that many of the kids in our truck had immaturely pointed and laughed. Tragically, to them it has become commonplace to live so close to violent, anonymous crimes.

On our way back home several hours after having passed by the almost-Easter crime scene, we cautiously stopped by a corner store near our home to inquire about the victim of the murder. (It is, however, extremely important not to get too involved in the details, fall into gossiping or finger-pointing when such a crime occurs. If your comments reach the wrong ears the perpetrators might target you as the next victim in order to silence you.)

Darwin asked who the victim had been (and not why he had been killed or by whom), and the shop owner let out a belly laugh and pointed to a house a few doors down and said in an unnecessarily loud voice, "It was Barney! They took him out! ¡*Qué lástima!*"
He shook his head and continued laughing about his neighbor's tragic murder as Darwin and I stared at him, surprised and deeply saddened by his total lack of empathy.

Darwin excused us from his presence. We were politely on our way, and we continued driving onward toward home, again in silence.

The victim in question was a man we had seen and greeted on occasion. He was the young adult live-in boyfriend of a notorious middle-aged woman about whom we have heard many terrible rumors.

. . .

A few days later, I was again in our old white pickup truck, but this time alone. I had been running errands in our town before rumbling back up that gravel road to our ranch. I drove past the home of the man who had been murdered. I sensed a sudden and unmistakable impression from the Lord was pressed upon me in regard to the woman who survived him: *Go console her.*

I was squarely in front of her home when I received the unexpected instruction, but the car continued in motion for almost a block as I considered the command. I felt surprised and at the same time excited that the Lord had so clearly spoken to me, but I began to reason that it would just be too much of a hassle to turn the car around at that point. Oh, my excuses are so weak! It would have been nice to go console the woman whose live-in boyfriend had just been murdered — it was, in fact, what Jesus probably would have done — but maybe another day. Or maybe never.

The car kept rolling up that gravel road — farther and farther from her home as I tried to reason my way out of obedience — when I finally turned the car around, retraced the path on which I had come, and parked right in front of her small, one-story cinder block home. God had won. I breathed deeply — praying that the Lord would give me the right words and that He might open the woman's heart to receive from Him. I got out of the car and approached the twig-and-barbed-wire front gate.

Most people in our rural town recognize my husband and me as the directors of our little school and know generally that we are doing Christian work in our neighborhood, but there are still many people whom we don't know personally.

This woman was one such case, as we had passed by her home just about every day and waved to her as she hand-washed her clothes in her front yard or as her children played on the porch, but we had yet to take the next step to really get to know one another. (Although last year we were tempted to break the ice by storming over to her home to rebuke her for the harmful and potentially illegal influence she was having on several of our teenage male students.)

One of the woman's teenage daughters let me in. Several little children and a few young adult women were hanging around in the small living space and suddenly stared at me, waiting.

The command I sensed the Lord had impressed so undeniably upon me was, *Console her*. It was not, *Confront her about whether or not she has been selling drugs to the neighborhood boys and tempting them sexually*, nor even, *Share the gospel with her*. I remembered this as I asked the Lord once more for direction in the stillness of my own heart. I was convinced He wanted me to console her, regardless of who she was and what she had done.

The woman in question suddenly appeared from around the corner. I began, at once totally sure, "I believe God directed me to come here to visit you. My husband and I heard about what happened to Barney, and we are really sorry..."

She drew near and sat next to me on the small couch without any physical or emotional barriers between us as if we were old friends. I put my hand on her knee affectionately. I asked her how she felt and reiterated several times that my family and I were very sorry for her loss. Trust was quickly established between us as I listened to her, and she began sobbing freely as I reached out to embrace her in a comforting hug. I felt like I was consoling Queen Bee or Roller Coaster in one of their moments of adolescent emotional crisis, but this time it was our precious, broken neighbor at least a decade older than me.

After twenty minutes or so of consoling her in this way, I offered to pray for her if she should feel comfortable with me doing so. I knew she was not a Christian. She eagerly agreed much to my surprise, and I held her hands in mine and prayed that, in His timing, God might grant her salvation, peace, and transformation in Christ for His glory. I did not expect God to do anything in that specific moment, but I trusted He could bring her to repentance and saving faith by His own methods in His own timing.

Throughout the entire encounter all of the young people around us observed quietly and intently. At the time of my departure I hugged several of them. They were visibly surprised to receive such a display

of affection from a stranger. I left with joy in my heart, believing
that the Lord had undeniably done something there.

A couple weeks passed, and I was in our car with a group of our
teen foster daughters and local students on an evangelistic outing.
Thus far everything was going very well as the young women
were going door-to-door offering to bless our neighbors with
a provision of food and pray for those who were willing to receive
prayer.

We were coming to the end of our journey when we passed in
front of the woman's house whom I had visited and consoled. She
was not on our list to visit, but she exited her twig-and-barbed-
wire gate and approached me while I sat in the car. I greeted her
warmly, and she asked if I could share a Bible with her because she
had just begun going to church and was now seeking the Lord. My
eyes grew wide.

As our teen girls exited the last official house on our route,
I informed them that I felt like God was leading us to one
more home: that of my new friend who had asked for the Bible.
Several of our girls seemed hesitant and others downright scared,
as this woman's negative reputation is pretty well-known in our
neighborhood. Her teenage daughters had even publicly insulted some
of our foster daughters and local female students on several occasions
as they'd walked peacefully by their house.

This would definitely be a powerful lesson for our girls in loving
their enemies as Christ taught us to and praying for people who
don't fall into their category of "family" or "best friends."

The girls looked at me as if to ask, *Are you sure?* and I assured
them that she would be open to prayer and that she had recently
begun seeking the Lord. I would wait in the car because I wanted
them to learn to serve as Christ's messengers without an adult
constantly doing the talking and praying for them.

As they began walking toward that same twig-and-barbed-wire front gate I had passed through a couple weeks prior, I whispered to my Daredevil who was toward the back of the group. "She needs a lot of hugs. *Asegúrate de que le des uno.*" I winked at my beautiful daughter, and the look in my eyes encouraged her not to be scared. I prayed that my girls might learn to share His love with a woman few people draw near to.

I waited in the car a long time before all of our girls came filing out from within the woman's house. Their expressions had changed drastically and now reflected great measures of peace and joy. They piled back into the car with me as they lovingly bid farewell to the woman whom they had been so reluctant to visit.

Pulling away from her home, I turned around in my seat to ask one of our local students how the experience had been. She beamed and answered, "*Todo salió muy bien, gracias a Dios.* She was really open to receiving prayer. Several of us prayed for her. At the end, we each took turns giving her a hug, and that really touched her. I think she needed that."

I smiled and thanked God in my heart as we rumbled back up that long gravel road to our ranch, the car now empty of the sacks of food it had held, but each young woman full of a profound experience of Christ's love in and through them.

Losing My Marbles in a Big Way

July 31, 2019

I slammed our white metal kitchen door with all my might and bent over on our empty front porch, my fists clenched as I let out a blood-curdling scream. I walked away from our home as fast as I could, and my open palm found our empty school building's front door as I slammed into it several times before letting out another prolonged barbaric cry. In a blur I made my way across our empty front yard, hot tears streaming down my bright red cheeks. I didn't look back and only stopped walking once I reached a spacious grassy area behind our little purple office building, hidden from the world. I shook all over and streams of sweat began spilling out over my body as the intense emotions had provoked my fever to break. My teary eyes contemplated the towering mountain range before me, just beyond our fence. A bone-gnawing class of sorrow pounded within me, and I struggled to contain it.

I, the household peacemaker and mediator who so diligently strives to cultivate a quiet, respectful home atmosphere and who feels jarred to the core every time a door gets shut unnecessarily loudly, had utterly lost control.

I had been inside our simple cinder block kitchen with wire mesh windows and bright orange walls only moments prior. I had reached my flash point and slammed my palms down on the table I had been sitting at with my husband and our teenage foster daughter Roller Coaster. In one fluid motion I stood up and overturned the table. Such violent behavior wasn't like me at all, and I knew I had to get out of our home so as not to inflict more damage.

As I stood shaking and crying behind our empty office building, physically removed by a couple hundred yards from our home and completely out of eyesight, no neat, structured prayers came to mind. I tried to pray, but the waves of sorrow within me blocked out any possibility of mental focus.

Then, suddenly, a figure appeared from around the corner, walking calmly straight toward me. My husband.

I knew he would come. I glanced between him and the ground at my feet several times, unsure what he would say to me after such a violent display. Neither he nor I had ever behaved in such a way. We had never made a habit of yelling in our home, even in the tensest of moments. He looked neither angry nor sad; he embodied the peaceful stability of God's love. If I had lost my marbles (and I had in a very big way), he had all of his in a perfect little row, organized by color and size.

He reached me and, still without saying a word, wrapped his arms around me in a safe, loving gesture. I shook ever harder in his strong embrace, and I sobbed, "I'm so sorry. I didn't mean to overturn the table on you … I'm just so sad, and I can't take any more lies and deception *No entiendo todo lo que está pasando.*"

Feeling the huge beads of sweat all over my arms, face and neck, he observed in a whisper that my fever had broken. We both knew I had been in yet another grueling bout with Typhoid fever for the last several weeks. He quietly assured me, "*Tranquila, amor.* I know you're sad. I am too."

We stayed in that position for a really long time, me heaving and sobbing in his arms in a remote corner of our ranch property as the sun began setting. Teenage Daredevil appeared unexpectedly from around the corner with a black trash bag in her hands, keeping a respectful distance from us as she pitched the bag into the large metal trash recipient several yards away. I'm sure she didn't have to take the trash out at that exact moment; I'm convinced she wanted to see what kind of exchange Pa and Ma were having after the embarrassing kitchen showdown. As quickly as she had appeared, she disappeared around the corner in the waning light, without saying a word.

I confessed in my husband's loving embrace, "I just wish I could make the right decision for them. It's so sad and so scary to see the path they are choosing, and I know we can't stop them. We've already tried in so many different ways. I love them and want them to choose God's best for their lives. I don't want them to leave, Darwin. *Son nuestras hijas.*"

My husband expressed similar sentiments, as we had both had our hearts on the chopping block for the past several weeks in the increasingly tense atmosphere of our home. That afternoon my husband and I had been sitting around our kitchen table with Roller Coaster, trying to lovingly confront her about a serious infraction she had committed for the umpteenth time. Rather than confessing, however, our beloved daughter began spewing one lie after another out of her mouth. Enduring several minutes of this had just been that last, seemingly insignificant straw that broke this weary camel's back. I couldn't take any more lies.

Roller Coaster, our newest foster daughter who had come to form such an important part of our lives only a few months ago, along with Queen Bee, the eldest of all of our children and one of the first three to move in almost six years ago, had gone headlong into a dangerous turmoil of rebellion like we had never experienced before in our household, culminating in their desire to leave our home altogether.

My heart ached, not for our loss but for the deep suffering I could foresee in store for both of our precious treasures if they followed through with their current plans for a life founded on licentiousness and "freedom" from God. My heart ached especially for young Roller Coaster, as in a few short months she and I had formed a special bond. Even in the midst of many daily trials I could sense in her such enormous potential and a sweet innocence begging to be recovered in Christ. Why did it all have to end this way?

My husband and I knew, however, that we could not keep them at home and on track by force. Not even Jesus tried to coerce, plead, or impede those who desired to abandon Him. He simply spoke the truth in love, offering the opportunity at eternal life to all those who might believe and obey while letting go those who wished to live according to their own terms.

Our home is not a jail or a youth detention center, after all, but rather a delicate living organism like any other family. In years past we had emphatically gone after Distance-Keeper who had run away twice, trying to convince her through tears to return home. Following such emotionally taxing search-and-rescue missions, my husband and I had tried to will the rest of our children to stay at home under ours and God's protection as long as possible for their own good. We had a strong notion of what would await them in Honduran society if they tried to prematurely begin "adult" life without a completed education and stable place to live. We were, however, losing the battle, at least with these two.

The storm within me losing speed, my husband and I walked in perfect silence hand-in-hand back across our front lawn. He opened our kitchen door for me (the one that I had exited and slammed an hour or two prior), and I walked in, unsure what I would find.

Someone had returned the table to its normal position and reestablished kitchen order. I later found out that Daredevil and Tender Heart had taken care of the mess. Our kids had already eaten dinner. I went into my room for a while before decidedly going into each of our kids' rooms to embrace them and wish them goodnight, as my husband and I do every evening. The act felt forced and uncomfortable as much for me as for them after all that had occurred that afternoon, but I went through with our evening ritual nonetheless. In that exact moment, all I wanted to do was return to my room with as little interaction or emotional demand as possible and get the day over with.

Less than a week later, Queen Bee and Roller Coaster left home. They both dropped out of school, bid us a nearly emotionless farewell and walked out our front gate in broad daylight with all the belongings they could carry, intent on taking on the world on their own terms, not ours or God's.

Our hearts shattered in a million pieces, but we didn't try to stop them.

And, while my hand's violent encounter with the schoolhouse door left bruises that lasted well over a week, the open wounds of my heart would take much longer to heal.

Hand–Washing in a Mosquito-Infested Yard

October 28, 2019

For the past three months we have been discovering a new "normal" in our household in the absence of our daughters Queen Bee and Roller Coaster. After a period of mourning we cleaned out and repainted the empty room they left behind and now use it as a small family den and prayer space. I've personally gone from grief to anger to sadness and back again many times, but even in the midst of it all we feel real, deep peace in our household. Actually, our home has never before enjoyed such exceeding levels of calm and harmony.

More than anything, I've been left wondering what role, if any, I am now to play in our lost girls' lives. Has my involvement as "Ma" come to an utter and abrupt end forever, or is there hope of communication and an open window for influence that will reappear on the horizon at some point? My husband Darwin and I, after all, weren't ready to throw in the towel. In many ways I feel like I am still hanging on to it real tight. Nevertheless, I know that normal life must go on.

So, this morning I rolled out of bed and began the process of preparing to wash. It had only been three days since I last washed, but our laundry basket was overflowing already.

My husband was single until he married me at age thirty, so he had many years of experience hand-washing his own clothes. While in this culture many "macho" men think that washing is strictly a woman's job, my husband has a humble heart and does help from time to time when I am sick or overburdened with other tasks. (And I'm pretty sure he washes a whole lot better than I do.)

In my first several years on Honduran soil, I struggled mightily with dedicating so much time to such a household chore that — to me — is anything but spiritual and revolutionary. I would much rather spend my time doing something "important"! I have, however, learned to humbly accept my fate and even embrace the outdated activity of hand-washing clothes.

I sighed. It is currently the rainy season in Honduras, which on the whole brings tremendous blessing. The rains water the fields and fill the rivers (although not entirely, due to frightening levels of deforestation). The downside to the rainy season, however, is that the clothes hanging on the line don't dry as quickly and hordes of hungry mosquitos arrive on the scene.

Standing in my bedroom in nothing but my bra and underwear, I sprayed every inch of my body with insect repellent, knowing that as soon as I stepped outside dozens of potentially disease-porting mosquitos would come swarming around me. Even my ears, forehead, cheeks, and chin were lathered in bug spray. I then put on an old, thick pair of sweatpants and an XXL t-shirt that many years ago was my dad's. If I stepped outside in sandals or barefoot, the mosquitos' first target would be my feet and bare ankles, so I put on my husband's tall black rain-boots.

I was as prepared as I could be, so I began the process of hauling all our dirty laundry outside in various large plastic washing bins, gathering the bag of detergent, bleach, and so forth. As I stepped outside into our little side yard where our *pila* is situated, sure enough I was greeted by countless buzzing mosquitoes.

From there, I spent the next two hours happily hand-washing the contents of the large plastic laundry buckets. My mind wandered as my hands washed; I contemplated growing Chopping Block's surprising success under her loving aunt's care. We had made the hour-long drive out to see her again recently on one of our periodic visits. She's shot up like a weed and is now a blossoming, albeit awkward, preteen, still lightyears behind mentally. Her aunt joyfully bragged to us how obedient and helpful Chopping Block was in the home. I had bitten my lip and thanked the Lord in my heart for Chopping Block's smooth adjustment to life with her dedicated aunt; after all, she had rarely been obedient with us and had not reached the point of being helpful in our home! Surely the Lord has blessed Chopping Block's sweet aunt in a special way for her goodwill toward her quirky, broken niece.

I took out a pair of my husband's jeans and began removing grass stains with our coarse washing brush. My mind followed other bunny trails under the bright morning sun. I finished up the last of the clothes, our guard dogs faithfully following me to and fro as I walked from the *pila* to the clothesline and back again. I felt a very real sense of contentment bubble up within me upon completing such a simple but gratifying task.

I re-entered our home mid-morning, by then soaked from the waist down and my rain boots squeaking across our tile floor. I quietly greeted our five treasures who were still in the process of shaking off their slumber. Shadow Puppet and Tender Heart laid out peacefully on our living room couch reading while Calm Sea contentedly practiced music. Fireball went about sweeping each room in our house; Daredevil came up alongside of me to give me a warm hug and a good-morning smile.

I thanked God in my heart for this new day and for His blessing of peace over our ever-evolving patchwork family.

Hope Postponed
at the Pier

November 22, 2019

Perhaps unlike many in today's world, I am not particularly
enthralled by social media. I opened up my first Facebook account
about a decade after it became popular and have intentionally
abstained from many of the other social media outlets that populate
the web. I prefer old-fashioned email to Twitter. I can even happily
survive several days at a time without being "connected". I still find
joy in the simple pleasure of crafting hand-written letters and sending
them via the post office.

Nevertheless, I am thankful that my virtually dormant account on
Messenger has proved a useful tool in keeping in touch with Roller
Coaster who left our home four months ago.

After a period of uncomfortable silence, she sent word that she
wanted to connect with me online. I eagerly obliged, and thus
a cyber relationship was formed between us a few weeks ago. She
asked forgiveness several times for her behavior, noting that her
leaving was not our fault but hers. After a few weeks of loving
and consistent communication we decided to meet up in the city to
see each other.

I arrived several minutes early and began nostalgically walking
the pier that overlooks the Caribbean Sea. A half dozen fishermen
of various skin colors sat perched on the edges of the recently
renovated pier; a couple kissed passionately, and others meandered
about in small groups and took photos. The sky above was clear and
the weather pleasant. My mind wandered and I imagined what my
meeting with Roller Coaster might hold. I had been praying about
this encounter for several days (and for her in general for months).
In my heart of hearts, I clung to the hope that she would want to
return home with us.

I glanced far down the pier toward the shore and saw a figure
walking toward me. She was too far away for me to distinguish
her facial features, but by her gait I knew instinctively who it was.
I smiled and waved high in the air to test my hypothesis. The figure
waved back enthusiastically, and several emotions sprang forth from
my chest. Would we be able to talk easily as we used to, or had our
relationship been strained beyond repair?

When we reached the same spot mid-distance on the pier, we
embraced in a warm, comfortable hug as we had done hundreds of
times in her few short months living in our home. She readily called
me "Ma", which caught me off guard and made me feel surprisingly
awkward. Had she not abandoned me as her surrogate mother
months ago, choosing to do life according to her own rules? What
did it mean that she still honored me with that title, or was it mere
habit, void of any real meaning?

I shook off my doubts.

Her adult female cousin and the woman's little daughter were in
tow, as Roller Coaster informed me that she had begun living with
her cousin's family several weeks ago. The woman looked to be in
her early twenties; thin, beautiful and of African descent, but her
eyes displayed no emotion whatsoever. I greeted her warmly, but
she failed to make eye contact or engage in any general pleasantries.

She sank down into a wooden bench near us as if she had already endured too much in her short life and stared off in the distance. I tried to include her in our conversation, but she seemed too tired or disinterested to make any effort. Her little daughter, the polar opposite of her mother, proved to be boisterous, bossy, and full of life. The mother made almost no move to interact with or set limits for her naughty little one.

Roller Coaster and I talked in fluid, comfortable fashion for nearly an hour as we sat on one of the many wooden benches on the pier. I could tell we still enjoyed considerable levels of trust and affection, and in many ways, I felt like she had never left our care. Her dress was much shorter than I would have allowed her to wear had she been under our care, but other than that she looked exactly the same. She asked eagerly about each of our kids and was interested to know how "Pa" Darwin was doing as well.

After several minutes of conversation, I ventured, "How is your relationship with God? Have you continued seeking Him on your own these past few months?"

She bit her lip and answered sincerely, no masks, "Umm ... Honestly I haven't continued in the things of God. *Me siento muy lejos de Él......*" Her gaze left mine as she began studying the sea just beyond the pier.

We both knew she had come to profess faith in Christ under our care and had asked to be baptized. Although she had experienced many ups and downs (hence her namesake), her faith had been sincere and the baby steps she had taken toward the Lord had been real. Her new faith was one of the biggest reasons her exit from our home had broken my heart. I knew that she could go live with her biological family (as she had) and that they would provide her basic needs of food, water, and shelter, but her spiritual needs would largely go untended.

Even as I tried to speak words of wisdom and direction into the life of precious Roller Coaster, I knew it wouldn't be enough. An hour of loving advice and prayer on a pier would ultimately do little to guide a life that is adrift on wild seas.

Our time came to its natural close, and I offered to drive them back home as they had made the long journey via a combination of public busses and walking. As they indicated where to turn at each point along the way, our old pickup finally pulled to a stop about an hour's drive from my starting point in front of a run-down one-story building that rented single rooms to entire families. A herd of unsupervised children ran about on the rocky, trash-littered front lawn that all the families in the dilapidated complex shared. The place was, in many ways, the epitome of developing world poverty.

I hugged Roller Coaster and her cousin good-bye. Her cousin's eyes just about bulged out of her head upon receiving my unexpected show of affection. Maybe it had been a long time since anyone (or at least a stranger) had given her a sincere hug.

As they shut the passenger door and I put the car in reverse, I couldn't help but feel a mixture of sadness and hope welling up in my chest. Roller Coaster had made no mention of wanting to return home. *Why, Lord? Surely You want to bring her home, right?* Maybe in our next visit she or I will breach the topic. Maybe all we need is time.

Remembering Home

December 20, 2019

Our Martian Child is all grown up, so I suppose we can now call him *Martian Man*. After a tumultuous season outside our home, once he turned eighteen we helped him jump through the necessary hoops to enroll in the Honduran military. He completed his basic training recently and asked if he could come visit us during his short leave before being assigned to his official post. Of course, we said yes.

We had sent him a care package a couple months ago and were in frequent phone contact with him. We continued to pray for him as a family, and of our other teens who had prematurely left home, he appeared to be one of the only ones interested in still having a relationship with us. We were thrilled to be his long-distance support network during this new chapter of his life. He still called us "Pa" and "Ma", and even after all we'd been through the mutual respect and affection between us were tangible.

Martian Man came walking through our front gate, visibly content and exuding a sweet, humble confidence. He was home. We all went out to greet him. He looked stockier than before and walked with a swagger that might have been slightly embellished to impress us. He wore a t-shirt the military had given him and had his hair neatly cropped.

Over dinner, Martian Man had center stage; we gave him our undivided attention as he shared with us the range of his experiences during basic training. Yes, he sang to us in a thundering, patriotic voice each and every one of the dozen military songs he learned and, yes, he got up from the table more than once to demonstrate to us some advanced exercise routine they had put him through. As one hour gave way to the next and Martian Man showed no sign of slowing down, Tender Heart rolled her eyes and made a move to get up from the table. I reached out to stop her, telling her that we would all listen to everything Martian Man was enthusiastically sharing. Listening, after all, is an act of love.

She plopped back down, glancing at me with a You've-got-to-be-kidding expression, unimpressed by all of Martian Man's military bravado. She had clearly seen better things since sliced bread. I ignored her expression and kept listening to Martian Man, who had taken no note of Tender Heart's boredom. I thought in my heart, *Oh, Tender Heart, if only you knew how proud we are of him.*

As we received the unabridged version of Martian Man's basic training triumphs, most of our kids and even Darwin and I began to droop slightly in our chairs. When he finally took a deep breath, we took advantage of the small pause to announce family prayer time. Certain times of prayer in our home are mandatory; others are optional. This particular occasion would be optional.

We patted Martian Man on the back and thanked him for having let us into his exciting new world. My husband and I began heading to our family's prayer den without necessarily expecting him to follow. We knew he had had a long day and must be tired, plus we still weren't sure how actively he continued to practice his faith.

We took our places on a couple old foam mattresses that we had covered and sprinkled with mismatched pillows. It was kind of like a long, cozy L-shaped couch on the floor. Tender Heart, Calm Sea, and Daredevil came through the doorway to sit among us.

Martian Man, too, appeared and took a seat. Our prayer den was new to him, but his face displayed a sweet eagerness to participate and draw near to the Lord. Eyes closed and heads bowed, we each took turns praying out loud, and Martian Man was no exception. He'd never been particularly eloquent with words, but his raw honesty and humble faith before the Lord deeply touched my heart.

After prayer we walked him to his old bedroom with Shadow Puppet and gave him a goodnight hug just as we had done with all of our other kids. Through his budding facial hair and developed, muscular body I could see a radiant, innocent joy in his eyes. To me he was still the twelve-year-old lost boy whom we took in on a whim of faith.

He got up before dawn the next morning as he commented to us that he had become accustomed to such an early schedule in the military. I sensed Tender Heart scoff as she walked past. She had long-since reached her limit on his never-ending "in-the-military" comments.

Moments later, I sat on the couch in our living room, lacing up my boots as I silently studied Martian Man. He was sitting quietly at the piano bench across the room from me, looking at the black and white keys.

He had never been a particularly gifted musician as Queen Bee had been, but he had managed to learn to read basic sheet music and even tap out a few happy tunes on the piano. We used to laugh because whenever we had a visitor, he would run to the piano to begin playing the one or two repetitive tunes he knew. Alas, if Darwin wanted to get Martian Man to practice piano, we had to invite guests over so our quirky son could feel he was impressing them!

His calloused, semi-uncoordinated hands began touching the keys lightly, the beautiful instrument still silent. I could tell he was trying to recall the notes. Then at once he began to play with total confidence, much to my surprise. He remembered. His theme songs burst forth in our family's little living room as I continued to watch him. He seemed oblivious to all that was around him as he played for several minutes virtually without error.

Then, abruptly, he stopped. Sitting silently on the piano bench, his eyes began tracing the dozen or so framed photos that were squeezed like sardines on top of the old piano. Many of the pictures were of him. Our precious macho-man looked deeply moved as his eyes studied intently one photo after the next, a precious tune welling up within him. He began singing softly in his deep, manly voice one of the Christian hymns we used to sing every Sunday at our missionary mentors' home.

This time he didn't sing to impress anyone; I believe he was singing in genuine thanksgiving to the Lord. Tears welling up in my eyes, I thanked the Lord in my heart. *Our son hasn't forgotten. The seeds that were sown in him have not been lost. Thank you for bringing him home, Father.*

Never Felt That Kind of Love Anywhere Else

January 2, 2020

I glanced at the calendar hanging on our bright orange living room wall. In just a couple weeks' time we will begin our seventh year of directing the little school that we operate out of our ranch home. What we initially began with three students has grown over time, although it has never been our goal to have "bigger" but rather "deeper." While many organizations and churches might equate large numbers with success and significance (and small numbers with failure and insignificance), we are convinced that God has given us a different perspective. We actually fight to keep our mission small and are hesitant to expand to include the masses.

Roller Coaster has continued in surprisingly open communication with us since my meeting with her on the pier several weeks ago. Our other kids are weary about us recovering our relationship with her. After two suicide attempts under our roof, they know first-hand how demanding it was to live in close confines with her, but nevertheless my husband Darwin and I hold out hope of her return to the safety of our nest.

At Roller Coaster's request, a few days ago I sat on the dilapidated and graffitied front porch of the small complex where I had dropped her off after our visit at the pier. I was perched on the broken cinder block half-wall as Roller Coaster and her glossy-eyed cousin, nearly lifeless just as I had seen her a month prior, sat on mismatched plastic lawn furniture. I asked if I could pray before we began in order to put our meeting in the Lord's hands from the get-go, and they both accepted. As our prayer came to a close, I opened my eyes to see a middle-aged man with the appearance of a street thug entering the small run-down room that Roller Coaster lived in with her extended family. The man eyed Roller Coaster with a grin that sent chills down my spine, and the provocative glance she returned to him made my stomach churn.

I began as lovingly and directly as possible, eager to get Roller Coaster out of this unhealthy environment, "Well, Roller Coaster recently sent me a message saying that she is interested in returning home to live with us, so I am here to discuss that possibility with you both and lay down the general guidelines that my husband and I have established."

Her adult cousin half-smiled warmly, although she still gave off the impression of being a million miles away. I could tell she loved and supported Roller Coaster even in the midst of her own material poverty, but I wondered what real depth there was to the bond between them. She nodded lethargically toward Roller Coaster, prompting her to speak her mind. She began, "Yeah, Ma, I'd really like to move back home with you and Pa Darwin. The love I felt there I've never felt anywhere else. *Aquí, con mi familia–*" she shook her head in genuine frustration, as if remembering all the verbal fights and threats she had told me about between her and her mother "–*no es lo mismo.* There's no peace here, and I've drifted far from God."

Then Roller Coaster continued, catching me off guard as I thought she had already finished. "And that's why, Ma, I really want to go back home to your house for a month until things settle down here."

For a month? One month? Any hope that had been growing within me got swept up and carried far, far away in an instant. I could do no more than stare at her blankly for a moment while my heart crashed to the floor, trying to adjust my expectations to her extremely short-term understanding of family.

I want you to come home to us, forever, to be our daughter and to grow whole. That doesn't happen in a month, Sweetheart; it takes years, maybe even a lifetime. I could not deny the disappointment that threatened to engulf me.

From that point on, our conversation was a numb blur to me. I felt I came to identify a little bit more with her empty shell of a cousin, although I'm sure for different reasons.

Sucked dry after nearly an hour of going round and round, it was increasingly clear that I would be unable to convince her to make a permanent move. I embraced Roller Coaster warmly and likewise bid my affectionate farewell to her cousin before heading for the car. To avoid making an impulse decision, I encouraged her to think and pray about our offer of hope and a future. We would check in with her in two weeks to hear her final answer.

Well, my husband and I didn't have to wait two weeks to hear from her. Just a couple days after meeting with her, she sent us a short message informing us that she would be declining our offer in favor of staying where she was.

The image of the thug with lustful eyes for our Roller Coaster slithered uninvited into my mind, and my heart broke for our daughter who had once more chosen the chaos of a life of "freedom" (sexual or otherwise) over a life full of peace, blessing, and life in Christ. We all knew this was her final answer, as we had told her we didn't want to serve as her last-resort emergency line when things got complicated with her biological family. We would not be willing participants in her game of back-and-forth. Over the coming years she would reap what she sowed, and her decision — for better or worse — would pay dividends that she would be responsible for.

I stared sadly at my husband as we both sat propped-up in bed in the late evening. We had just received the news of Roller Coaster's final decision. I felt as if a large door had been prematurely shut in our faces all over again, that Roller Coaster herself had shut the door that we believed God had opened to lead her to healing and salvation. We felt engulfed in sadness — not for ourselves but for our daughter who had chosen to remain lost even as God was calling her home — and we faintly considered the fact that our relationship with her had, in fact, come to an abrupt, unsettling end.

Stoned in the Street

January 11, 2020

It was Saturday morning, and blossoming teenage Fireball was waiting for a good friend of hers to arrive at our ranch to spend the day together. After waiting several minutes, Fireball politely asked if she could call to see why her friend had not yet arrived. Absent-mindedly going about my daily domestic chores, I handed Fireball my cell phone without giving the situation a second thought.

Moments later, Fireball approached me with a strange expression on her face, my small, simple cell phone in her hand, hanging limply by her side. She informed me, "My friend told me she was unable to walk all the way up the gravel road to our home because it's been blocked off and they're not letting anyone pass."

I furrowed my brow and began processing aloud, "Well, that's strange." Our ranch lies on the outskirts of our rural town, and there is never much traffic in our neck of the woods. Although it is fairly commonplace for protesters to close off the bridges or more populated roads from time to time, in our experience no one had ever bothered to close off the lonely one-lane gravel road leading up to the mountains.

Fireball continued, *"Ella me dijo que hay un cadáver tirado en la calle."*

"A dead body in the street?" My eyes grew wide and my heart picked up speed. Who had been killed so close to our home, and why? Why do these kinds of violent acts keep happening so frequently around us?

I borrowed my husband's more advanced phone and sent a quick message to a trusted neighbor who might know something. I figured simply asking the identity of the victim was considered within the safe, appropriate range of questions.

The rest of our busy household carried on with their morning routines without a care in the world as I hovered over my husband Darwin's smartphone, which laid idly on the top of our living room's piano next to our family photo albums and piles of unorderly sheet music. I stared at the screen with shaky hands, waiting for a response. I hoped against hope that it had all been a big mistake, that Fireball's friend had misinformation.

Ding. Our trusted neighbor answered, stating in as few words as possible who had been the victim: Skinny Guy.

Nicknames based on physical appearance are extremely common here, and as you might imagine there is more than one "Skinny Guy" in our area. After all, nicknames such as Fat Guy, Whitey, Black Guy, Big Nose, Hairy, Baldy, Curly Girl, Blue Eyes, and Chubby Cheeks are all too common in our area and oftentimes threaten to push a person's real name onto the brink of extinction. Whatever distinguishing physical characteristic you have, it seems like people use that (with or without your permission) to form your nickname, and it often sticks for life. No joke.

However, when I received the message my heart sank because I sensed I knew exactly which "Skinny Guy" was the victim. I sent a couple clarifying messages using the legitimate name of the young man in question as tears began to swell in my eyes. Regardless of which "Skinny Guy" it was, it was a terrible tragedy.

Ding. Ding. My hands clasped the edge of the piano as I steadied myself; the identity of Skinny Guy had been confirmed. It was exactly who I thought it was. Further details were also offered up: he had been stoned to death by an unidentified group of people the night before, his mangled body found dead this morning. Hence a group of concerned neighbors blocked off that portion of the narrow public road perhaps for lack of a more effective action to take.

I left the phone on top of our old wooden piano, clenched my hands into weak fists and slipped out of our bustling living room. I isolated myself for several minutes in the humid, cave-like bathroom that connects to the sleeping quarters I share with my husband. I stared at myself numbly in our small bathroom mirror as tears spilled down my red-hot cheeks. My body shook, and I bit my lip, hoping no sounds would escape. Mourning, I prayed silently, if such raw, nearly wordless sentiment can even be considered a prayer: *Oh ... Why so much violence? When will it stop? Oh, Lord......*

I wearily fought back the unsolicited torrent of mental images, fed by my vivid imagination: Skinny Guy struck down by numerous flying rocks, eventually too bloody and weak to stand, possibly finished off by a few acute blows or maybe left to suffer a slow death alone under the night sky. I had no idea who had committed the crime or why, but my mind went wild imagining all the possible ways his stoning could have occurred.

I cried harder as I stood alone in our muggy bathroom, considering numbly the fact that we had visited Skinny Guy at his home only a few days prior to give him a homemade holiday cake with a sincere, hand-written note of encouragement. Skinny Guy had stared at my husband in genuine disbelief as he reached out over his short front gate to receive the unexpected gift. I will never forget the serene, surprised look in his eyes as he thanked my husband for our family's kind gesture. It was as if his bad reputation had fallen away if only for a moment, and he appeared to me as an innocent, open child. I remember thinking, *Maybe no one has ever done something like that for him because most people are scared of him. I feel like we're gaining ground, Lord. Maybe all we need is more time to keep extending to him Your love in action...*

A dear local friend of ours had invited Skinny Guy to an in-home Bible study on numerous occasions, and my husband and I had likewise invited him to join our school to finish his basic education. Just a couple months ago a group of our students had made a house visit to pray for and speak biblical truth to him individually, and they came away from the encounter feeling encouraged about the possibility of going back. It seemed like we were always on the verge of a breakthrough with him.

Skinny Guy was, after all, a notorious leader among our town's rogue youth and someone whom many people actively feared. To us, however, he was just one more person made in God's image and in need of His grace. I remember seeing him almost every day as we would jog through our neighborhood as a family. In the beginning, he was visibly surprised when I would wave at him and smile kindly, but over time he began freely returning the neighborly gesture.

I grabbed the edge of the wooden dresser in our small, stuffy bathroom as my head fell forward slightly. In the midst of my grief I tried to regain composure. I didn't want to draw unwanted attention from our kids for my splotchy cheeks and bright red, swollen eyes. I breathed deeply, shook my head as if it were a matter of merely freeing myself from a few pesky cobwebs and determined in vain to suppress the storm of sadness and rage within me.

As wrong as it may sound to someone who has never lived in this culture, I willed my trembling heart to grow a few more callouses around it as I thought, *If I'm going to make it here over the long-haul, I can't let each tragic murder get to me. I have to know these kinds of things are going to happen, and I can't spiral downhill each time they do. Get your act together, Jennifer. Shake it off.*

With that I dabbed my teary eyes with a little wad of toilet paper, breathed deep and re-entered our living room as if nothing had occurred. By then my husband and all of our children held the same information I did, and the environment in our household had shifted slightly. Some of our more sensitive kids looked a bit shaken; others did not.

Tender Heart approached me as I was fumbling in my purse for my keys. She stroked my back and tilted her head to one side, asking sweetly if I was okay. It was obvious that I was not, but nevertheless I nodded without saying a word, as I feared the floodgates would burst open if I dared say anything. Determined to keep moving, I smiled politely at her and headed out the front door as we all made our way to our old Toyota pickup truck. We would drop by Fireball's friend's house to pick her up on our way into town.

As my husband drove down that one-lane gravel road, I sat silently in the passenger's seat looking out the window. Our car was forced to take a slight detour, but nevertheless I could see our normal route clearly enough through the window: about a dozen neighbors stood around the crime scene idly, indeed blocking off the road. Thankfully I could not see the body, but I knew it was there.

Although this tragic act of violence occurred a mere mile from the local police station, not one police officer could be found on the scene of the crime, even hours after a crowd of neighbors had been gathered there.

My thoughts turned somber as our old Toyota pickup sauntered on in respectful silence: Skinny Guy's brutal murder was just one more uninvestigated, unpunished crime. He was one more soul violently taken from this world, most likely unready to stand before God's throne. Would anyone even bother to write an official report to mark the devastating end to another human life?

A Visitor at the Gate

July 18, 2020

It was early afternoon, and I was sprawled out on our double-sized bed in one of those rare moments home alone on our ranch. My husband Darwin had generously offered to take our five treasures to a local river for an afternoon of healthy play in nature. While I had other plans on my agenda for my quiet afternoon at home, I ended up drifting off into a blessed miracle nap after having suffered another nearly sleepless night.

My nap didn't last long, however, as I was jolted from my shallow sleep by a loud, shrill voice just outside our gate. I rubbed the sloppy drool off my cheek and squinted my eyes uncomfortably, wondering for a brief moment if I could pretend no one was home and ignore the seemingly friendly — or desperate? — visitor who had dropped by so unexpectedly. So much for an afternoon home alone, I thought.

After a few moments of indecision, I got up and peered hesitantly through the window — it was Queen Bee. She stood just beyond our gate, her posture denoting expectancy. She had filled out slightly and was dressed modestly. Later this year she will be turning twenty; I will be turning thirty.

I paused in the window, unsure why she had come. She had already been in our home the day prior to attend our youngest child's — her biological brother's — thirteenth birthday party. We had invited her to attend the intimate family event, although we were admittedly hesitant about how the affair might go. This month had marked her one-year anniversary of living outside our home, and throughout her time away we didn't need even five fingers to count the times we had seen her face-to-face. Even though she continued living in our small town, our interactions with her had been brief, sparse, and tense, all on neutral territory. Inviting her to Shadow Puppet's birthday party in our home was a risky move, but by God's grace her participation in the celebration had gone better than any of us could have imagined or hoped for.

My husband and I had witnessed in her a newfound maturity and humility, beautiful and unprecedented. Her smile was not fake but contagious; she earnestly encouraged her younger siblings in a nurturing way. She seemed genuinely glad to be in our home and freely expressed this to us several times. She wore no masks and held no hidden agenda. She spoke sincerely about her counseling sessions with a local pastor and how the family that took her in several months ago holds frequent Bible studies, in which she actively participates. Between birthday party activities, she and I even sat down at the piano together for several minutes, enjoying a passion we both used to share. Everything had been like a fresh start granted to us directly from the hand of God. In a very real way, we felt that God was beginning to answer our prayers, as much for our eldest daughter's transformation in Christ as for the restoration of our relationship with her.

Why had she returned today without notice?

Still trying to shake off my groggy state from my interrupted nap, I opened our front door and waved big right as she was about to give up and leave. She perked up when she saw me and waved back. I greeted her with a tired smile and asked if everything was okay. She smiled big and told me she was just stopping by to drop off a bag of still-hot homemade bread.

As I approached our front gate to receive the warm, unexpected gift, I knew that in Honduran culture this could mean only one thing: the beginning of a friendship.

CPSIA information can be obtained
at www.ICGtesting.com
Printed in the USA
LVHW020751010621
689025LV00004B/166